INTRODUCING
NEW TESTAMENT THEOLOGY

by the same author

ACCORDING TO JOHN
BIBLE AND GOSPEL
DESIGN FOR LIFE
THE EPISTLE TO THE ROMANS
GALATIANS TO COLOSSIANS
THE GOSPEL ACCORDING TO SAINT MARK
THE GOSPEL ACCORDING TO SAINT PAUL
INTERPRETING THE PARABLES
INTRODUCING THE NEW TESTAMENT
THE WORK AND WORDS OF JESUS

Introducing
New Testament
Theology

A. M. HUNTER

SCM PRESS LTD
BLOOMSBURY STREET LONDON

334 00699 6

FIRST PUBLISHED 1957
SECOND IMPRESSION 1963
THIRD IMPRESSION 1966
FOURTH IMPRESSION 1969

© SCM PRESS LTD 1957

PRINTED IN GREAT BRITAIN BY
NORTHUMBERLAND PRESS LIMITED
GATESHEAD ON TYNE

CONTENTS

PREFACE

A DOZEN years ago the SCM Press invited me to write a short Introduction to the New Testament. This little book, which was kindly received, is being published this year in a much enlarged edition. But, since it first appeared, I have been cherishing the dream of adding to it a companion volume which would handle the theology itself, and not simply questions of Introduction. My dream is now fulfilled in the present book.

Not another one (do I hear somebody saying)? Have we not had in the last two decades a number of New Testament Theologies? Yes; but mostly by Germans, and mostly big ones beyond the purse and sometimes the learning of the ordinary minister and interested layman. Besides, as Callimachus said long ago, *mega biblion mega kakon*, a big book can be a big bore . . . So I have tried to serve my busy brethren by providing them with a brief study which, I hope, will put them *au fait* with the latest theological insights and emphases. Let no one fault me for not exhausting the subject. This was not my aim, as it is far beyond my gifts. But I have tried to handle the salient issues and to discuss the chief New Testament theologians. (I am interested particularly in their unity, but I have also tried to bring out their diversity.) Part I is headed 'the Fact of Christ' and treats of the Kingdom of God, the Ministry of Jesus, and the Resurrection. Part II, which is entitled 'the first Preachers of the Fact', shows how the men of 'the Twilight Period' (A.D. 30-50) proclaimed the Fact. Then in Part III we meet the chief 'Interpreters of the Fact': St Paul, St Peter, the Writer to the Hebrews, and St John.

7

I have no hope of pleasing the pundits who will give my little book a superior smile and reach for Bultmann or Stauffer. But it may help the hard-working parson who wants to keep up to date theologically, and the theological student in our Church colleges may value a short and simple Introduction to a very big subject. Is not this one of the things that Divinity professors like myself are for?

I should like to acknowledge gratefully the valuable help I have received from two friends, Mr Ian Howard Marshall, M.A., and the Rev. Robert H. Mounce, B.D., M.Th., in the reading of the typescript and the proofs.

A.M.H.

April 1957

PROLOGUE

THE Bible is the Book of the People of God; or, if dynamic terms are preferred, the Book of the two Exoduses.

The Old Testament recounts the story of God's choice of Israel to be his People: how he rescued them from Egyptian bondage through Moses and made a Covenant with them at Sinai, whereby they became the People of God (the first Exodus) and how through the succeeding centuries he led and guided them by 'his servants the prophets', disciplining them for their high destiny by blessing and by judgment, and kindling in their hearts the hope of a Day when he would crown his gracious dealing with them in the happiness of the Messianic Age.

The New Testament is the story of the fulfilment of the Divine Plan of Redemption. It tells how God completed his saving Purpose by sending his Son the Messiah and inaugurating his Reign in his Ministry, Death and Resurrection. This is the Second Exodus (cf. Luke 9.31), and this is the event we call 'the Fact of Christ'. By this phrase we mean the totality of what Jesus Christ's coming involved, his person, work and words, of course, but also the Resurrection, the advent of the Spirit and the creation of the new Israel destined to become the Catholic Church.

And if it be asked what is our warrant for regarding the Bible in this way, our answer must be that it is the best of all warrants. It is Dominical. So Jesus saw the whole story of redemption—as witness his parable of the Wicked Vine-dressers (Mark 12.1-12). Only if we see the Bible thus, can we take seriously his words: 'Think not that I came to

9

destroy the law or the prophets: I came not to destroy but
to fulfil' (Matt. 5.17).

The historical setting of the Fact of Christ may be briefly
noted. It begins with a baptism administered by John the
son of Zechariah in the river Jordan, midway through the
reign of the Roman Emperor Tiberius. Among the
recipients of that baptism was a man generally known as
Jesus of Nazareth but sometimes as the son of Mary. Born
in Bethlehem of Judea, about 6 B.C., in the reign of the
Emperor Augustus, while the *Pax Romana* girdled the
world, he had grown up in Nazareth of Galilee, accompany-
ing his parents to the festivals at Jerusalem, and learning the
trade of a carpenter. We know that as a young man he had
acquired a name for his skill in expounding the scriptures,
and we surmise, from his later words and habits, that,
though friendly to all, he loved to withdraw from the haunts
of men into places of solitude for meditation and prayer.
When the great Augustus died in A.D. 14, he must have
been about twenty years of age. Doubtless the news of the
Emperor's death troubled many of his contemporaries, fearful lest it might mean the end of the Augustan peace and
an orderly empire. But Jesus was thinking of another peace
and another empire, and biding his time. When, a dozen or
more years later, the voice of prophecy, long silent, rang
out again in the Judean wilderness through the lips of John
the Baptist, Jesus knew that his time had come. He went
down from Nazareth to Jordan to be baptized by John and
to begin a Ministry in which he would proclaim a Kingdom
mightier than the Roman and tell of a world saved not by
man who became God (like Augustus or Tiberius) but by
God who became man. For he himself was this Man,
and the stage was being set for the second and greater
Exodus. . . .

NOTE ON SOURCES

THE 'Fact of Christ' calls for a study of the Kingdom and the Messiah in the Synoptic Gospels. Why do we exclude the Fourth? Not because we dismiss it as a theological interpretation which loses all touch with the facts of history. It is sometimes assumed that 'interpretation' necessarily means imposing some alien meaning on these facts. It may equally well mean drawing out their true implications. This we believe St John did, as we believe his Gospel contains much more good history than was once supposed. Yet difference there is between the Fourth Gospel and the first three. It may be thus expressed. Whereas the Synoptists set the theology in a historical framework, St John sets the history in a theological framework (as witness the Prologue). A difference only of degree, perhaps, but a real one, and our justification for numbering St John among the Interpreters of the Fact.

As for the Synoptic Gospels, we regard them as reliable historical documents. This is not to claim that everything in them (e.g. certain incidents found only in Matthew) is true. But it is to claim that, when used in accordance with the methods of a sane and moderate criticism, they provide a trustworthy account of what Jesus said and did, and to repudiate the radical conclusions of critics like Bultmann of Germany. In this country it is a principle of justice that a man is innocent until proved guilty. So we may regard the works and words attributed to Jesus in the Synoptics as authentic, unless cogent arguments are adduced to show that they are not so.

Part One

THE FACT OF CHRIST

I

THE KINGDOM OF GOD AND THE MINISTRY OF JESUS

PARADOX lies deep at the heart of the Gospels. It is the paradox of the relation between the Kingdom of God and the Ministry of Jesus. Yet on the understanding of this paradox depends our understanding of the whole New Testament.

What is the dominant theme of the Synoptic Gospels? This question, scholars agree, has only one right answer—the Kingdom of God.[1] With this theme Jesus began his preaching; it is the theme of his parables; it is the theme on his lips at the Last Supper. In the thought of the Kingdom of God he lives, and works, and dies.

Consider the earliest Gospel. St Mark, after relating the mission of the Baptist, goes on to tell how Jesus came into Galilee announcing, 'The Kingdom of God has arrived.' And yet, as we read on, the story which unfolds itself is of a man, Jesus of Nazareth, who calls himself indeed 'the Son of Man', apparently stressing his humanity. This Jesus, after

[1] The statistics are these. Mark has 'the Kingdom of God' fourteen times and Luke thirty-two. In Matthew 'the Kingdom of God' occurs four times and 'the Kingdom of Heaven' (which means the same thing) thirty-three times.

being baptized by John, proceeds to preach and teach and heal, first in the synagogues and later by the lakesides in Galilee, until he has won such a reputation that, after a great open-air meal with his followers, they are fain to sweep him off and make him a king.[1] At this point, for some not very clear reason, Jesus retires from Galilee to the north-west boundary of Palestine. When he returns to the neighbourhood of Caesarea Philippi, there is some secret talk between himself and his twelve disciples about the Messiah, the Son of Man and death; and, six days later, a mysterious incident on a mountain-top. Then, as if having taken an irrevocable decision, Jesus moves south with his disciples to Judea and Jerusalem. There, about Passover time, after cleansing the Temple, he is arrested by his enemies, tried, condemned and crucified, one of the Twelve having 'turned King's Evidence' against him. A few days later, the friends of the crucified man are announcing that he has risen from the dead. . . .

This, briefly, is Mark's rather puzzling story. How can this be the story of the Kingdom of God? The very phrase suggests all the power and glory of God being exhibited in such a royal way that all may know that he is God. Yet all we see, apparently, is a Galilean prophet uttering the truth as he understands it and sealing his testimony with his life's blood, as many a Jewish prophet had done before. What is the explanation of this paradox? Can it conceivably be that the career of this Galilean prophet is the Kingdom of God?

Obviously, our first summary is jejune and inadequate. There are things in the story—hints and happenings pregnant with profound meaning—which we have missed, and, missing, have failed to understand the story. Let us try again, this time seeking to bring out these important things.

[1] John 6.15. John makes explicit what is implicit in Mark's narrative.

I

Let us start with the Baptism of Jesus. The story of what befell Jesus at Jordan, like that of the ensuing Temptation, must have come to the disciples from Jesus himself; for, according to Mark, nobody else saw or heard the really important happenings there. What were they? First, a voice from heaven said to Jesus as he rose from the water, 'Thou are my beloved Son; with thee I am well pleased.' Highly significant words when we realize that they come from Ps. 2.7 and Isa. 42.1. One is the coronation formula of the Messianic King of Israel; the other the ordination formula of the Servant of the Lord. This remarkable combination cannot be fortuitous. It was his own destiny that Jesus saw in the Messianic King and the lowly Servant of the Lord. At his baptism Jesus was made aware that he was called of God to be the Servant Messiah, that he 'was born to suffer, born a king'.

The other extraordinary event at the baptism was his vision of God's Spirit descending on him. Again, we are reminded of Isaiah's Servant: 'I have put my Spirit upon him' (Isa. 42.1). What does the descent of the Spirit mean? It means that from this time on Jesus knew himself to be 'the anointed of the Spirit' (cf. Luke 4.18 quoting Isa. 61.1). We tend to think of the Holy Spirit as genial light; the Bible thinks of it as creative, almighty power, power in which God is acting. The descent of the Spirit therefore means his equipment with Divine power. Here we may find the secret of that manifest note of 'authority' which is to inform his later words and works.

If we were to put the meaning of the whole event in one phrase, would it not be 'The ordination of the Servant Messiah'?

II

Passing over the Temptation,[1] let us study next the words
with which Jesus opened his ministry in Galilee: 'The time
is fulfilled, and the kingdom of God has drawn near
[arrived]; repent and believe in the Gospel' (Mark 1.15).
Properly understood, these are startling words. It is a proclamation that men are living in a quite unique moment of
history, and that God is initiating a new era in the record of
his dealings with them.

Kairos, the Greek word here translated 'time', means the
appointed time. What time determined in the counsels of
God is this? References in the context to the Reign of God
and to good tidings (gospel) show that the clue is to be found
in Isa. 52.7 (cf. Isa. 40.9 f.). Half a millennium before, Isaiah
of Babylon foretold the return of the exiles. He saw them
coming back in triumph to Jerusalem with God in their
midst and a herald preceding them with the good tidings.
All Jerusalem is pictured on the walls when suddenly on the
hill-top the herald is seen:

> *Look, 'tis the feet of a herald*
> *Hastening over the hills*
> *With glad, good news,*
> *With tidings and relief.*
> *Calling aloud to Zion,*
> *'Your God has become king!'*

Isaiah expected this day of God's Reign to dawn soon.

[1] See T. W. Manson, *The Servant Messiah*, 57. He points out
that in each of the three temptations 'the Messiah is invited to take
the centre of the stage in one form or another. Each time the
response of Jesus puts God in the centre of the stage, and the
implication is made clear: even the Messiah is only God's Servant
—indeed, just because he is the Messiah, he must be pre-eminently
God's Servant'.

However, in God's Providence, the stream of this great hope was to run underground for five centuries till 'the appointed time was fully come'. It came in the reign of the Roman Emperor Tiberius when Jesus appeared in Galilee, saying, in effect: 'The time which Isaiah prophesied has come.'

If the first incident said, 'This is the Ordination of the Servant Messiah', the second says: 'God has begun to reign'.

III

Consider next the Galilean Ministry itself. We have tended to think of it as a time of quiet teaching and preaching in contrast with Jesus' later career in Judea when he is marching on the Cross—the time of his Passion which we might equally well call his Action. But we misunderstand this earlier time if we picture it only as a peaceful pastoral wherein the serene wisdom of the Teacher accorded well with the flowers and birds of Galilee. Such a picture we obtain only if we scale down the miracles, interpret the parables as charming stories about moral commonplaces, and evacuate the eschatological sayings of their mystery and depth. Something of Whittier's 'Sabbath rest of Galilee' there may have been in the Ministry, but more of Bunyan's 'Holy War', the war against the powers of evil in which there fights for us

> the Proper Man
> Whom God himself hath bidden.[1]

We ought to picture the Galilean Ministry dynamically, not statically, and polemically rather than pastorally. 'Jesus', observes Goguel, 'did not say, "I am come to teach" but "I am come to kindle a fire in the earth".'

[1] Luther.

His words bear this out. He begins his Ministry by announcing that he is sent to 'proclaim release to the captives' (Luke 4.18). He compares his mission to the binding of the strong man (the devil) by a stronger (Luke 11.21 f.). To the returning Seventy he cries, 'I saw Satan fall like lightning from heaven' (Luke 10.18). His parables (as Jeremias has said) are weapons of war and his 'mighty works' signs that the issue is being victoriously joined with the powers of evil. And all through his Ministry there rings a note of terrible urgency, as though a crisis uniquely fraught with blessing or with judgment for 'this generation' were upon them (Luke 12.49-59, 13.1-5).

Only if we see the Galilean Ministry thus, do we see it aright; and the emergent picture of the Chief Figure in the campaign, so far from being that of a high-souled teacher patiently indoctrinating the multitudes with truths of timeless wisdom, is rather that of the strong Son of God, armed with his Father's power, spear-heading the attack against the devil and all his works, and calling men to decide on whose side of the battle they will be. 'No man, having set his hand to the plough, and looking back, is fit for the kingdom of God' (Luke 9.62). 'Leave the dead to bury their own dead, but go thou and proclaim the Kingdom of God' (Luke 9.60). 'The Kingdom of God is in your midst' (Luke 17.21). 'The Kingdom of God exercises its force' (Matt. 11.12). 'If I by the finger of God cast out demons, then is the Kingdom of God come upon you' (Luke 11.20). 'Behold I cast out devils and perform cures to-day and to-morrow, and the third day I am perfected' (Luke 13.32).

Our third study therefore shows us the Kingdom of God at war with the kingdom of evil, with Jesus spear-heading the attack. Looking back at the Ministry, many years after, St John saw it even so: 'The Son of God was manifested that he might destroy the works of the devil' (I John 3.8).

IV

Let us pass now to Caesarea Philippi (Mark 8.27-33). The Ministry has climaxed in 'the Galilean Lord's Supper', at which, clearly, popular excitement was running very high. Thereafter, probably in flight from the dangerous enthusiasm of his friends, Jesus has withdrawn to the north-west border of Palestine (Mark 7.24). But the battle joined in Galilee must be finished in Jerusalem (Luke 13.32 f.). So, before he moves south, Jesus makes sure that his disciples understand the issues at stake. In the solitude of Caesarea Philippi, he asks: 'Who are men saying that I am?' They reply that popular speculation takes various forms. 'But you,' he says, pressing the question closely on the disciples, 'what do you think?' At once Peter utters the thought in all their minds, 'You are the Messiah'. The right answer? Yes, and Jesus tacitly accepts it, but he goes on: 'The Son of man must suffer and die before he triumphs'.

Observe, he uses the title 'the Son of man', not 'the Messiah'. Was this the first time he had employed it? We cannot be sure. What we can be sure of is that the Son of man is not, as we once supposed, merely a poetical synonym for 'man'. On the contrary, it was 'about the most pretentious piece of self-description that any man in the ancient East could possibly have used'.[1] (If we translate it 'man', we must capitalize it as 'Man'). For 'the Son of man', a title ultimately derived from Daniel 7.13, is a mysterious Man who receives a kingdom from God and is destined to reign as God reigns. With this majestic figure Jesus identifies himself; yet, in the same breath, insists that suffering and death await him, because God wills it so. To Peter, with his hope set on a triumphant Messiah, the very idea is unthinkable. He rebukes Jesus, only to be himself in turn rebuked with awful severity. Peter is conceiving Messiah-

[1] E. Stauffer, *New Testament Theology*, 108.

ship in man's terms, not God's. What Jesus means is this: 'You find the very thought of a suffering Messiah abhorrent, Peter? Yet this is the way God's Reign works, and, God's great vice-regent though I am, I must travel the road marked out for the Suffering Servant of the Lord. There is no other way, and you must be ready to share my destiny' (Mark 8.34).

Six days later, follows another incident (Mark 9.2-8) closely linked with Peter's confession, yet so mysterious that to this day we hardly know how to begin explaining it. On a mountain-top as he prays,[1] Jesus is transfigured with an unearthly radiance. From the unseen world appear Moses and Elijah, talking with him (Luke says) 'about the *exodus* (deliverance) which he must accomplish at Jerusalem: ' and the bewildered disciples hear a Divine Voice—the same which had spoken to Jesus at the Baptism—reassuring them: 'This is my Son, the Beloved (two Messianic titles): listen to him.'

Our fourth study therefore says: 'The last battle between the Kingdom of God and the Kingdom of evil must be joined; and it will involve the death of God's Messiah'.

V

Let us pass now to Jerusalem, to the Last Week, to the Last Supper.

Jesus has entered the Holy City in 'lowly pomp'. He has cleansed the Temple. He has also predicted its destruction. In a house at Bethany a nameless woman, breaking a precious flask of unguent, has anointed him for his death. Now it is Thursday night, and in the quiet of 'a large upper room' Jesus meets with the Twelve for a final meal together (Mark 14.22-25, cf. I Cor. 11.23 ff.).

To understand what follows, let us recall certain things.

[1] These Lucan details illuminate Mark's narrative.

If the occasion is a supper, let us recall that a supper had served Jesus as an image of the Kingdom of God (Luke 14.16-24). This particular supper, moreover, is being held on the eve of Passover—or is, maybe, the Passover itself. Now, the Passover commemorated the great act of God which initiated the first Exodus and led to Israel's being marked out as God's special People by a Covenant at Sinai sealed with blood. But Jesus, declaring that the Jews were no longer God's people, had, by word and deed, spoken of the creation of a new Israel. Yet, before this could be, the Son of man must die as God's Servant to redeem 'the many' (Mark 10.45), and his Passion he had likened to a 'cup' to be drunk, a cup in which his disciples might somehow share (Mark 10.38).

Now notice what he does. First, he takes a loaf and breaks it, handing it to the Twelve with the words: 'This is my body [which is for you]. 'Then he delivers the cup to them, with the red wine gleaming in it: 'This [cup] is the new Covenant in my blood'. And he bids them eat and drink. What does he mean?

By setting apart the bread and wine, Jesus is offering his disciples a pledge of the Kingdom of God soon to come 'with power' through his sacrifice. In describing the broken bread and the outpoured wine as his body and blood he is not only claiming, somehow, to embody that Kingdom, but is representing, in splendid symbol, that sacrifice of his own life for 'the many' which he is soon to accomplish in fact. By asking his disciples to eat and drink of the bread and wine, so interpreted, he is giving them (as Otto says)[1] a share in the power of the broken Christ.

The new Covenant (Jer. 31.31 ff.) which must be ratified by the Servant's Death (Isa. 42.6, 49.8 and 53) has been symbolically inaugurated and in a few hours will be sealed in fact and in blood. Then the work of the Servant Messiah,

[1] *The Kingdom of God and the Son of man*, 308.

begun in his water-baptism in Jordan, will be consummated by his blood-baptism at Golgotha, that baptism in whose virtue many will share.

Thus the fifth episode is essentially a prophetic acted sign by which Jesus says: 'I pledge you a share in the Kingdom of God soon to come with power by the Servant Messiah's death'.

VI

Let us take one last look at Jesus. Betrayed and arrested, he stands before the High Priest: 'Are you the Messiah?' asks Caiaphas. 'I am,' replies Jesus, 'and you will see the Son of man sitting at the right hand of Power and coming with the clouds of heaven' (Mark 14.61 f.).

It is Jesus' last unconquerable confession of faith in his mission, and he clothes it in words from Daniel 7.13 f. (with a phrase from Psalm 110.1). 'There came with the clouds of heaven', Daniel had written, 'one like unto a son of man, and he came even to the ancient of days, and they brought him near before him. And there was given him dominion, and glory, and a kingdom.' Thus, despite the apparent ruin of his cause, Jesus predicts his victory. What he predicts here is not a second coming to earth but vindication and enthronement. He will be received to the highest place that heaven affords, and this his exaltation and victory they shall know.[1]

In the last study Jesus therefore says: 'The Servant Messiah's triumph is assured'.

Was the Servant vindicated? Did 'the pleasure of the Lord prosper in his hand'? And did he 'prolong his days'?

We shall discuss the Resurrection later. Meantime, let us see how the Story of Jesus looks after this series of studies.

[1] On this saying see J. A. T. Robinson, *Twelve New Testament Studies*.

We have tried to fill in the bare outline with which we began, dwelling on 'the hints and happenings pregnant with profound meaning' and interpreting them with a 'depth exegesis'.

As a result we are driven to two very important conclusions:

(1) We cannot tell the Story of Jesus without bringing theology—and especially eschatology—into it. Without the theology it does not make sense. And the key to most of the theology is in the Old Testament, especially in the Servant Songs of Isaiah and the seventh chapter of Daniel.

(2) The second conclusion is no less important. Our studies have made two things clear:

(a) Jesus believed the Kingdom of God to be present in himself and his Ministry—present in a 'mystery' (Mark 4.11), indeed, but none the less really and dynamically present.

(b) No less clearly he saw his Messianic Ministry, from Jordan to Golgotha, as a fulfilling of the prophecies of the Servant of the Lord.

The result of putting (a) and (b) together is a terrific paradox, a paradox which, we know, gravely perplexed the disciples and indeed only became luminous after the Resurrection. Time and time again Jesus tried to initiate them into its truth, supremely on the road to Jerusalem, as witness Mark 10.42-45. What he was trying to let them into was the Messianic Secret—the secret not of *who* Messiah was (they had guessed this) but of *what* he must do and suffer.

But the secret, the mystery—what is it? In technical terms, it is that the meaning of 'realized eschatology' and the meaning of the Messianic Ministry of Jesus are one and the same. In simple terms, the career of Jesus as the Servant Messiah, from Jordan to Calvary, *is* the Kingdom of God, God acting in his royal power, God visiting and redeeming his People. For the Kingdom of God is no earthly empire to be set up by a political *coup d'état*. It is a Kingdom in which God rules redeemingly through the Ministry of Jesus: not something added to the Ministry, but the Ministry itself. The suffering and sacrifice of Jesus, the Servant Son of man, so far from being only a prelude to the triumph, are the triumph itself, a triumph which the Resurrection will clarify and reveal.[1]

Two generations after, St John saw this clearly when he depicted the Cross as 'the glory' of Jesus; but the first heralds of the Gospel were not blind to it when they said, in their preaching, that in the Ministry, Death and Resurrection of Jesus the Kingdom of God had come:[2]

> The kingdoms of the world go by
> In purple and in gold.
> They rise, they flourish and they die
> And all their tale is told.
>
> One Kingdom only is Divine,
> One banner triumphs still,
> Its King a Servant, and its sign
> A gibbet on a hill.[3]

[1] See T. W. Manson, essay 'Realized Eschatology and the Messianic Secret' in *Studies in the Gospels* (ed. D. E. Nineham), 209 ff.

[2] The apostles' proclamation was: (1) The prophecies are fulfilled. (2) The New Age has come with the Fact of Christ. (3) Therefore repent and believe.

Jesus' proclamation had been: (1) The time is fulfilled. (2) The Kingdom of God has come. (3) Therefore repent and believe.

In both proclamations (1) and (3) are the same. What about (2)? The proclamation of the Ministry, Death and Resurrection of Jesus the Messiah has replaced the proclamation of the Kingdom of God. Could anything show more clearly the truth of our conclusion?

[3] From *In hoc Signo* in *Through the Christian Year* (Bradby and Hunkin).

2

THE GOSPEL OF THE KINGDOM
OF GOD

THE Ministry of Jesus, we saw, is the inauguration of the
Kingdom. We propose now to draw out the implications of
this paradox and to support them with evidence.

1. *The Kingdom of God is present in the Ministry of Jesus*

Few phrases have been so abused as 'the Kingdom of
God'. We must begin therefore by purging our minds of all
modern misunderstandings. The popular idea is that it
means some sort of earthly Utopia to be built by men on the
basis of Jesus' teaching. Others take it as a kind of Biblical
equivalent for the evolutionary process, on the principle
of 'some call it Evolution, and others call it God'. They
forget that, for the fulfilment of history, the Biblical writers
look not so much to a process of evolution from within as
to a divine intervention from without. A third tendency, as
old as Augustine[1]—the tendency to equate the Kingdom
with the Church—is no less mistaken; for it confounds the
Divine Rule with the people who live under it. Similarly,
the Liberal view of the Kingdom as the rule of God in the
hearts of men (and so men's obedience to God's will) con-

[1] This is the modern R.C. position. The Kingdom of God is to be
identified with the Church, and we need not ask which one. Thus
R. A. Knox in his *New Testament Commentary*, Vol. I, 58, writes
'The kingdom of heaven means, as usual, the Church'.

fuses human response with Divine activity. God's Reign exists, however men respond. It claims the obedience of men truly; but it is there before the claims are made, and it is still there if men reject them.

To understand the phrase in the Gospels, we must remember that it means, linguistically, *the kingly Rule of God* and that it implies the Biblical idea of God, the God who acts, whose workshop is history and who is working out a great and gracious purpose in it to an appointed end. Our first thought of the Kingdom must therefore be *dynamic* and in terms of God's acts in history. Our second must be *eschatological*. In ordinary speech the word 'eschatology' usually means beliefs about post-mortem pains or pleasures. The Jews understood it differently. For them, eschatology meant the doctrine of the End—the End conceived as God's age-long and final purpose destined to be realized in the future and to give meaning to the whole travail of history.

Now, in Jewish thought, the Reign of God, so conceived, is this End. It is the great hope of the future for whose realization the pious Jew prayed (and still prays), 'May God establish his kingly Rule during your life and during your days, and during the life of all the house of Israel' (The *Kaddish* Prayer).

So understood, the Kingdom of God is another name for the Messianic Age (or the Age to Come) and connotes the whole salvation of God.

The Kingdom is thus primarily 'God's seed' rather than 'man's deed'. It is God regnant and redeeming. It is his Reign becoming manifestly effective in human affairs. It is God visiting and redeeming his People, as he had promised long ago.

If this accurately summarizes what the Kingdom of God means in the Gospels, we may see just how startling was the news with which Jesus opened the Galilean Ministry. 'The appointed time has fully come. The Kingdom of God has arrived.' It was nothing else than the news that 'the one far-off Divine Event' for which they prayed, had projected itself into history. What was formerly pure eschatology was now there before men's eyes, the supernatural made visible.

Nowadays we call this 'realized eschatology', and though 'inaugurated' might be the better epithet, the phrase contains essential truth.

Ever since C. H. Dodd coined it, arguing that the Greek verb in Mark 1.15 (*ēngiken*) has the force of '*arrived*', a linguistic battle has raged, Dodd's critics contending that 'is at hand', not 'has arrived' is the true translation. We believe that Dodd is right and that *ēngiken* here has the same force as *ephthasen* in Luke 11.20.[1] Even those who boggle at this translation[2] usually concede the main point, that Jesus believed the Kingdom to be a present reality in himself and his Ministry. Indeed the evidence of the Gospels leaves us no option.

To begin with, what is the sense of saying that 'the appointed time has fully come' if in fact the Kingdom is still round the corner? But there is a good deal more to add.

In one passage after another Jesus declares that the Kingdom of God has arrived:

'If I by the finger of God cast out demons, then the Kingdom of God has come upon you' (Luke 11.20. Q.).

'From the days of John the Baptist until now the Kingdom of heaven exercises its force'[3] (Matt. 11.12; cf. Luke 16.16).

---

[1] See W. R. Hutton's article in *The Expository Times*, Dec. 1952, in which he argues convincingly that 28 out of 32 examples of *engizo* in the Synoptic Gospels and Acts may reasonably be rendered 'come to' or 'arrive'.

[2] e.g. Vincent Taylor, *St Mark*, 167.

[3] Otto's translation (*The Kingdom of God and the Son of Man*, 108 ff.) taking *biazetai* as a middle voice, not as a passive ('suffereth violence'). The papyri have many examples of this absolute use of *biazomai* in the middle.

'The Kingdom of God is in your midst'[1] (Luke 17.21, L.).

'The tax collectors and harlots are going into the Kingdom of God before you' (Matt. 21.31 M.).

Not only so, but elsewhere Jesus unmistakably sounds the note of fulfilment:

'Blessed are the eyes which see what you see! For I tell you that many prophets and kings desired to see what you see, and did not see it, and to hear what you hear and did not hear it' (Luke 10.23 f. Q.).

'The queen of the south will arise at the judgment with the men of this generation and condemn them; for she came from the ends of the earth to hear the wisdom of Solomon, and behold, something greater than Solomon is here' (Luke 11.31. Q.).

'Go and tell John what you have seen and heard: the blind receive their sight, the lame walk, lepers are cleansed and the deaf hear, the dead are raised up, the poor have good news preached to them. And blessed is he who takes no offence at me' (Luke 7.22 f. Q.).

Here, with Jesus' reply to John in mind, we may consider the place of miracles in the Ministry. It is worth noting at the start that almost one-third of the earliest Gospel, Mark (209 verses out of a total of 661), deals directly or indirectly with miracle. Moreover, as far back as we can go in the Gospel tradition, we find it recorded that Jesus worked miracles—healed men's souls and bodies, recalled them from death and was credited on occasion with an extraordinary power over nature itself. On the human side, Jesus set great stress on the power of faith and prayer; on the divine side, he attributed his mighty works to 'the finger of God' i.e. the Divine Spirit working in all his plenitude through himself (Luke 11.20). If

[1] R.S.V., T. W. Manson, J. Weiss, K. L. Schmidt, W. G. Kümmel, etc.

then the Story was told from the beginning as the Story of one who worked miracles, what are we to make of them, and what place do they have in the Ministry of Jesus?

Once, men argued that, since the miracles were interruptions of the sacrosanct order of nature, they could not have happened. Nowadays, he is a bold man who affirms that nature is a 'closed system', and no self-respecting scholar dares to expunge the miracles from the story of Jesus. Some may well make him pause before accepting them as they stand. He may explain the Feeding of the Five Thousand in sacramental terms, discounting the miraculous element; or he may say that the Cursing of the Fig Tree is an acted parable of judgment which the tradition has transformed into a miracle. He will also make due allowance for the fact that the Jews had no doctrine of 'secondary causes'. But even when he has decided that this or that miracle in the Gospels may not really have been so miraculous as it seems, he will find it hard to deny that most of the healing miracles (whatever he make of the nature miracles)[1] are entirely credible in a story which, according to the records, ends with an empty tomb.

Why then did Jesus perform miracles? We know that he refused to 'give a sign' (Mark 8.12; cf. Matt. 4.5 f. 26.53; Luke 16.31): that is, to support his claims by some mighty act of thaumaturgy. He did not over-value the miraculous, and had no ambition to appear in the role of a mere wonder-

---

[1] H. E. W. Turner, *Jesus, Master and Lord*, 181, thinks the nature miracles should be put in a theological 'suspense account', i.e. we do not at present have the means of understanding them (though we might at any moment discover them). The question in our minds should be: Is Jesus the sort of person to whom such a mastery over nature can reasonably be ascribed? Dare we assign limits to the control he might exercise in areas beyond what we know of nature?

worker. Nevertheless, quite clearly—as witness his reply to John the Baptist's question—Jesus did regard his mighty works *as signs*—for those who had eyes to see. Signs of what? Signs of the presence of the Kingdom. The healing of the sick, the exorcism of evil spirits, the restoration of the maimed, the deaf, the dumb and the blind, the forgiveness of sins—all these were 'works' of the Kingdom. Not an addendum to his message but an integral part of it—'outgoings in power of the Love that was central to the Kingdom of God'. In one phrase, the miracles were the Kingdom of God in action.

Finally, the parables, in one way or another, concern the Kingdom and presuppose it as a present reality. They imply 'an eschatology that is in process of realization' (Jeremias). The parable of the Sower, picturing the ripe harvest-field, says: 'God has made a beginning. In spite of many failures the Kingdom of God comes at last'. The parable of the Seed growing secretly says: 'Put in the sickle, for the harvest has come'. The parable of the Leaven says: 'Like yeast in the dough, the Rule of God is working amongst you'. The parable of the Seine Net says: 'Like a drag-net, the Rule of God is gathering and sifting all sorts and conditions of men'. The parable of the Great Supper says: 'Come, for all things are now ready'. The parable of the Mustard Seed prophesies: 'The Reign of God, now like a small seed in your midst, will one day become a tree overshadowing the earth'.

All, observe, compare the Kingdom not to some dead, static thing but to something in movement,[1] to somebody doing something; and each of them says to those who have

---

[1] James Denney once met John Hutton in Glasgow on his way to preach and asked him what his sermon was to be. 'About the parable of the Leaven.' 'And the theme?' 'Oh, the quiet leavening influence of Christianity.' 'Hutton,' said Denney, 'did you ever see a piece of leaven under a microscope?'

ears to hear: 'God is among you in his royal power. Now is the day of salvation'.

2. *The King in the Kingdom is a Father*

When we say that the dominant theme of Jesus' preaching was the Kingdom of God, we easily forget that the King in his Kingdom was a Father. 'Father . . . thy Kingdom come,' he taught his disciples to pray (Luke 11.2). 'Fear not, little flock,' he told them, 'it is your Father's good pleasure to give you the Kingdom' (Luke 12.32). 'My Father appointed a Kingdom for me,' he said at the Last Supper (Luke 22.29). If the metaphors are mixed, only by mixing them can he reveal the truth. The in-breaking Rule of God is a fatherly Rule, and the manifested sovereignty a sovereignty of grace.

This is not to refurbish the old view that the message of Jesus was 'the Fatherhood of God and the brotherhood of man'. It is simply to insist that Liberal interpreters of the Gospel (like Harnack) did not err when they found Divine Fatherhood at its heart. But we cannot talk of it as they often did.

At one time men claimed that the new and momentous truth which Jesus came to declare was the Fatherhood of God. When they found that God was occasionally called the Father of his People in the Old Testament and that Jews of the first century A.D. sometimes addressed God as 'our Father', the claim had to be modified. The next step was to say that what Jesus did was to make the Divine Fatherhood a theological commonplace.

This is very wide of the mark, for:

(a) Jesus' name for the unseen Father was *not* the one used by his Jewish contemporaries. He called God *Abba* (Mark 14.36). (This Aramaic word probably underlies other passages where Jesus speaks of God as 'Father', 'the

Father' and 'my Father'.) Rabbinical sources show no parallel to this.[1] What research shows[2] is that *Abba* was the name Jewish children used in addressing their human fathers; but no God-fearing Jew would have dared to apply it to the holy God. The first to do this was Jesus, and, in default of other evidence, this word alone would testify to the uniqueness of his filial communion with God. The fact that Greek-speaking Christians took the word over into their prayer-speech points in the same direction.

(b) Jesus did *not* preach God as Father to the multitudes.[3] On his lips the Fatherhood of God was not a theological commonplace. He spoke of God as Father only to his disciples in private,[4] because the experience of God as Father was the supreme reality of his own life and because (as Plato[5] put it) 'to find the Maker and Father of this universe is a hard task; and when you have found him, it is impossible to speak of him before all people'.

(c) Jesus did *not* teach God's universal Fatherhood.[6] He spoke of God as his own Father, and taught that others might become his sons. But for this high privilege they must become debtors to himself. Not sons of God by nature, they might become sons by grace. The Johannine saying, 'No one comes to the Father but by me' (John 14.6) is confirmed by the Synoptic:

[1] See Strack-Billerbeck, *Kommentar* I, 393 f., II, 49f.

[2] See Kittel's discussion of *Abba* in the *T.W.N.T.* I, 5.

[3] For example, in the earliest Gospel, Mark, Jesus speaks of God as Father only four times, always to the disciples and always after Peter's Confession. The witness of the other sources, Q, M and L is similar.

[4] T. W. Manson, *The Teaching of Jesus*, chapter 4.

[5] *Timaeus*, 28 C.

[6] See H. F. D. Sparks's essay on the subject in *Studies in the Gospels*, 241-262, and compare Dodd, *Romans (Moffat New Testament Commentary)*, 130 f.

And no one knows the Father except the Son
And anyone to whom the Son chooses to reveal him.

(Matt. 11.27; Luke 10.22).

Here we may take the saying of Matt. 18.3: 'Unless you turn and become like children, you will never enter the kingdom of heaven'. 'Turn and become' means 'become again'. What did Jesus mean by people 'becoming again like little children'? It might mean 'become little again'; but the likelier interpretation[1] is: 'If you do not learn to say *Abba*, you cannot enter the Kingdom of God'.

To what conclusion are we led? Middleton Murry[2] once said: 'The secret of the Kingdom of God was that there was no King—only a Father'. This epigram contains truth. The King in Jesus' Kingdom was a Father—the *Abba* of his own prayer-life, the Father to whom he taught his disciples to pray for the coming of the Kingdom. But the knowledge of this Father was not a truth to be proclaimed from the house-tops or even revealed in parables except in hints, as in the great parable of the Gracious Father which we name 'the Prodigal Son'. Like Jesus' Messiahship, it was a secret disclosed to the disciples because it was the paramount reality of his own life and something of which he knew himself to be the sole mediator.

Only with the coming of the Holy Spirit did Jesus' secret about the Father become an *open* secret. Then the chief word in his esoteric speech became the precious possession of all God's adopted sons (Rom. 8.15 and Gal. 4.6). And since it is one thing to be a theist, quite another to be a son of 'Abba, Father', it summarizes, in four letters, the greatness of their Christian privilege.

[1] J. Jeremias, *The Parables of Jesus*, 133 f.
[2] *The Life of Jesus*, 37.

3. *The Kingdom of God implies a new Israel*

When men say (as they said not long ago) that Jesus never intended to create a church, they show that they do not understand what the Kingdom of God means. The idea of the *Ecclesia* has deep roots in the purpose of Jesus. His message of the Kingdom implies it. His doctrine of Messiahship involves it. His Ministry shows him creating it.

1. The burden of Jesus' message was that the kingly Rule of God had begun. But is God an *émigré* Ruler? And what kind of king is he who has no subjects? No more than any other rule can God's Rule operate in a void. It requires a sphere of sovereignty, a realm to work in. This is the reason why sometimes the Kingdom of God carries the secondary sense of 'realm' (as in the Beatitudes) and why Jesus can speak of men 'entering' the Kingdom or being 'cast out' of it. In short, the People of God is a necessary corollary of the Kingdom of God.

Not surprisingly therefore some of his parables clearly concern a community.

The parables of the Drag-net (Matt. 13.47 f.) and of the Wheat and the Tares (Matt. 13.24 ff.) suggest a society, comprising all sorts and conditions of men, in process of creation.

The parable of the Wicked Vinedressers (Mark 12.1-12) (based on Isaiah's older parable of 'the vineyard of the Lord of hosts which is the house of Israel') speaks of an Israel, old and new.

The parable of the Mustard Seed (Mark 4.30-32), with its reference to 'the birds of the air' recalling Dan. 4.12 and Ezek. 31.6, shows that Jesus has the gathering of a community in view.

But this is only the beginning of proof.

2. The correlate of the Kingdom is the Messiah, and it is quite clear from Jesus' conception of his Messiahship

that he envisaged a community. For Jesus interpreted his Messiahship in terms of two famous Old Testament figures —the Son of man in Daniel 7 and the Servant of the Lord in II Isaiah. Both these are *societary* figures. Just as the Son of man in Daniel represents 'the Saints of the Most High',[1] so the Isaianic Servant implies a community. If Jesus saw his destiny thus, he saw his Messianic task as the creation of a new Israel.[2]

If the point seems still doubtful, then let us note that Jesus spoke of himself and his disciples as a shepherd and his flock (Matt. 10.16, Mark 6.34, Luke 12.32). This is no mere pastoral picturesqueness. Not only was the Shepherd a common name in the East for a Divine Deliverer, but in two famous Old Testament passages (Ezek. 34 and Micah 5.4; cf. The Psalms of Solomon, chapter 17), the Messiah's work is described as the shepherding of God's flock. If Jesus calls himself the Shepherd, we expect him to gather his Father's flock. And this is precisely what he does in the Gospels.

3. We have been dealing, up till now, with the theological theory of the matter. Turn now to the Ministry, and we see Jesus translating the theory into practice.

First, he *called twelve men.*[3] It is the number of the tribes of Israel. To a Jew of any spiritual penetration this acted parable must have said, 'This is the Messiah and the new Israel'.

Secondly, he *taught* these men. Centuries before, Isaiah had formed a circle of disciples and committed his teaching

[1] The sect which produced the Dead Sea Scrolls not only thought of themselves as the true Israel but called themselves 'the saints of the Most High'.

[2] Cf. Mark 14.58 (John 2.19). This saying envisages a new shrine 'made without hands' for the worship of Christ's 'little flock'.

[3] The concern of the Apostles (Acts 1.15 ff.) to 'fill the vacancy' caused by Judas's defection shows that they regarded the number twelve as significant.

to them (Isa. 8.16-18). 'This,' says Robertson Smith[1] commenting on the passage, 'is the birth of the conception of the Church.' So it is now in the Ministry of Jesus. By appointing twelve men and instructing them, Jesus signifies his intention of creating a new People of God.

Thirdly, he *sent* them on a mission to proclaim the Kingdom. What was the mission's purpose? Let us recall that the Kingdom of God is something dynamic. It creates a people ruled wherever its power is felt. So Jesus' purpose becomes clear. It is the gathering of God's People. There is enough evidence in the Gospels to show that it did not fail.

Finally, in the Upper Room, by means of broken bread and outpoured wine, Jesus gave his disciples a share in the New Covenant to be inaugurated by his death. Long before, at Sinai, God had constituted the Hebrews into a People of God by making a Covenant with them. The New Covenant, now prophetically inaugurated in the Upper Room, implies the creation of a new People of God. Round the supper table that night the twelve sat as the nucleus of the new Israel.

We have said nothing about the two *Ecclesia* passages in Matthew (16.18 and 18.17), because they still lie under some critical suspicion. Without them our conclusion stands firm. The Kingdom of God implies the creation of a new Israel.

4. *The Kingdom of God involves a new pattern for living*

Our thesis here may be simply stated: it is that the ethical teaching of Jesus, of which the Sermon on the Mount provides a compendium, is his design for life in the Kingdom of God.

We should not be surprised that Jesus, the Herald of

[1] *The Prophets of Israel*, 274 f.

God's New Order, should also appear as a Teacher of Righteousness.[1] Eschatology implies ethics, and in the Bible the Divine Indicative usually carries with it a Divine Imperative. 'I am the Lord your God who brought you out of the land of Egypt . . . Therefore you shall . . .' So God spoke through his servant Moses when he set up the Old Order at Sinai. When now, through his greater Servant Jesus, he utters the new Indicative, 'The Reign of God has come', we expect a new Imperative. The ethic of Jesus is the imperative of the Kingdom of God. It provides a pattern of life for all who belong to the Kingdom which has come with the coming of Christ.

Albert Schweitzer, interpreting the eschatology in wholly 'futurist' terms, failed to make sense of the ethic of Jesus. He called it 'an ethic for the interim'. But you cannot dismiss the Sermon on the Mount—by common consent the sublimest utterance in history on the moral life—merely as a code of emergency regulations valid only for the few weeks or months that separate Jesus' preaching from Doomsday. Yet Schweitzer's phrase is not without its truth. It is an ethic for the interval—be it long or short—between God's coming in Christ and the final Consummation of all things.

The Beatitudes, which stand at the beginning of the Sermon and form its very soul, show how eschatology may go hand in hand with ethics. They are eschatological and messianic. Through them sounds the claim that 'the prophecies are fulfilled', that the Reign of God is here. What Jesus does in them is to sketch, in eight paradoxes, the spiritual portrait of the man of the Kingdom. What is not so often noticed is that the ethics of the Beatitudes are ethics of *grace*. Founded on the grace of the Father who gives the Kingdom to the child-like, they promise blessedness to all

[1] Cf. *Zadokite Fragments*, 8.10. 'Until there arises the Teacher of Righteousness in the end of the days.'

who, so far from advancing any claim (as of right) upon God, are content to be beggars before him and to trust him to provide all good things.

The six antitheses which follow in the Sermon set forth clearly the moral ideal of the Kingdom. Centuries before, Moses had delivered to old Israel God's will written in commandments. Now to the ancient 'It was said' Jesus opposes his messianic, 'But *I* say unto you'. But how much more radical are the demands of the New Order! The will of God for the New Israel as interpreted by Jesus the Messiah calls for truth in the inward parts, demands a morality in the blood and bone.

The old law said, No murder. *I* say, No angry passion.

The old law said, No adultery. *I* say, No lustful thought.

The old law said, Divorce on condition . . . *I* say, No divorce.

The old law said, No false swearing. *I* say, No swearing at all.

The old law said, Eye for eye. *I* say, No retaliation.

The old law said, Love your neighbour. *I* say, Love your enemy.

This is the moral ideal for the men of the Kingdom, the divine pattern at which they are to aim. It staggers us, as it must have staggered the first disciples of Jesus, by the terrifying height of its demands. If our salvation depended on our living it out completely in our lives, we might well say with Peter, 'Who then can be saved?' But though it is a pattern for real living,[1] and not a blue-print for Utopia, it is not a new code of law on the perfect keeping of which hangs our salvation. For the God who gave it is no dour driver of

[1] The teaching, so far from being legislation for an ideal world, implies the continuance of society as we know it—a society wherein you may get a blow on the cheek or have your coat stolen.

hard legal bargains but *Abba,* Father; and we are saved not by law but by grace.

Such, then, is the design for life in the Kingdom of God. What is the central, the distinctive thing in it all? Beyond question it is the commandment of love. In this commandment, says Jesus, all other commandments are subsumed and fulfilled (Mark 12.29-31). Love is the master-key to the morals of the Kingdom of God. By love Jesus does not mean some kind of sentimental emotion; neither does he mean that we must resolve to *like* certain people. (In this sense we cannot love to order.) Love, as Jesus defines it in saying and parable, means 'caring'—caring, practically and persistently, for all whom we meet on life's road, caring not merely for the worthy and deserving but for all who need our help, even enemies. This is the new 'law' of the Kingdom, because the King in the Kingdom is a Father who cares even for the ungracious and ungrateful and whose innermost nature is love.

5. *The Kingdom is centred in Christ*

When Marcion said, 'In the Gospel the Kingdom of God is Christ himself', he did not err. For, as we saw, the Ministry of Jesus—his career as the Servant Messiah—is somehow the Kingdom and the power and the glory. We must now study the point in more detail.

Consider, first, what we may call the Evangelists' evidence. Where St Mark writes, 'the Kingdom of God come with power' (Mark 9.1), St. Matthew changes it to 'the Son of man coming in his Kingdom' (Matt. 16.28). Again, where St Mark writes 'for my sake and the Gospel's' (Mark 10.39) St Luke has 'for the sake of the Kingdom of God'. (Luke 18.29). These are not wild and irresponsible changes. If the Evangelists saw fit to make them, they assumed an equivalence between the Kingdom of God and Christ.

To this we may add evidence from the usage of Jesus himself. It is significant that the Kingdom is promised only to those who attach themselves to Jesus' person, and that being discipled to him is equivalent to being 'in the Kingdom of God'. (See Mark 10.17-31 and Luke 9.57-62.)

Observe, next, the implication of such a saying as Luke 11.20: 'If I (*ego*: emphatic) by the finger of God cast out demons, then the Reign of God has come upon you'. There speaks One who knows himself to be the Rule of God incarnate and in action.

Consider, finally, the parables and beatitudes of Jesus. The Kingdom of God forms the theme of both, yet somehow the person of Jesus is always there in the background. If he says, 'Blessed are they that mourn, for they shall be comforted' (Matt. 5.4) it is as if he said, 'Yes, and I will be their Comforter' (The Comforter was one of Messiah's names).[1] If he tells them a parable of the Kingdom, like that of the Lost Sheep (Luke 15.4-7; Matt. 18.12-14), it is as though he said 'Yes, and I am God's Shepherd come to seek and to save the lost' (cf. Luke 19.10). When a parable speaks of the Kingdom, then Jesus is hidden behind the word 'Kingdom' as its 'secret content'. In short, both beatitudes and parables are burdened not only with the secret of the Kingdom but with the secret of Jesus. And the two secrets are, at bottom, one.

Why then is the connexion not made more explicit in the Synoptic Gospels? The answer lies in 'the Messianic Secret'. During his public ministry Jesus refused to proclaim himself as the Messiah, and only at the end, standing

---

[1] In our Lord's time the 'Comfort' prophecies of Isaiah (40.1, 61.2 f.) were referred to the Messianic Age. See Ecclesiasticus 48.24 where Ben Sira says of Isaiah:

'By a special inspiration he saw the last things,
And comforted the mourners in Sion.'

before the High Priest on his trial, did he openly avow his Messiahship.

Instead, as we know, he preferred to be known by the mysterious title of 'the Son of man'. Does this invalidate our point? On the contrary, this title holds the key to the connexion between Christ and the Kingdom.

The Synoptic Gospels contain about three dozen well-attested examples of this title on Jesus' lips. Usually it is clear that he is alluding to himself. Some of his uses are quite general; but, for the most part, they group themselves round two sharply contrasted motifs: suffering and sovereignty. What underlies Jesus' use of this title with these two motifs? For an answer, we must consider the origin of the phrase.

Nowadays most scholars agree that the source of Jesus' title is the vision in Dan. 7.13 ff. with, probably, some influence from the interpretation given it in the book of Enoch.[1] Now it is in Dan. 7 that we find the clue to the connexion between Christ and the Kingdom:

'And behold, there came with the clouds of heaven one like unto a son of man, and he came even unto the Ancient of Days, and they brought him near before him. And there was given him dominion, and glory, and a kingdom, that all the peoples, nations and languages should serve him.'

Then, after learning that the four beasts in the vision represent four kings, we read:

'But the saints of the Most High shall receive the kingdom and possess the kingdom for ever.'

'Son of man . . . the kingdom . . . the saints of the Most High.' In these related concepts, and the whole theology of history implied therein, lies the solution to our problem. God gives the Kingdom to the Son of man, and the saints of the Most High receive it.

---

[1] In *Enoch* the Son of man is an individual, pre-existent in heaven, and the designated Head of the People of God.

Now, if this be so, the Son of man in the Gospels is no mere periphrasis for man as man (as in Psalm 8.4) but the title of a heavenly person who receives sovereignty from God himself. When Jesus so styles himself he claims to be the Bearer of God's Kingdom to men, and in his Ministry we see that Rule embodied and in action. But this is not all. In Dan. 7 the Son of man represents 'the saints of the Most High'. He is the Head of the People of God. So we may understand why Jesus promises the Kingdom to those who attach themselves to his person and why he sets himself to create a new People of God.

But, it may be urged, whatever the Son of man may be in Daniel (or in Enoch), in the Gospels he is no triumphant figure. His sovereignty, if he has any, is veiled. Instead, we read that the Son of man must suffer and die before he triumphs. Why? It is because God has ordained that Jesus the Son of man shall fulfil the destiny of the suffering Servan of the Lord. It is by the *Via Dolorosa* that the Son of man must go to his throne.

If there is truth in all this, the connexion between Jesus and the Kingdom is established, and we can approve Marcion's dictum. But we are not quite done yet.

Think of God's New Order only as a Kingdom, and its Bearer may well call himself 'the Son of man'. But, earlier, we saw that for Jesus the King in the Kingdom was a Father. If he who rules in the Divine Kingdom is a Father, only one word will describe him who brings it to men. It is the word 'Son'. This is why the Gospels record that Jesus in a parable of the Kingdom (Mark 12.1-9) spoke of himself as the 'only son' of the Lord of the Vineyard, and why, talking with his disciples, he could make this stupendous claim:

' All things have been delivered to me by my Father,
And no one knows the Son except the Father,

And no one knows the Father except the Son,
And anyone to whom the Son chooses to reveal him.[1]

(Matt. 11.27; Luke 10.22, Q.).

'A bolt from the Johannine blue,' say the critics in incredulous surprise. Let us rather say: an authentic word from the lips of One who knew that Father as none other ever did. A filial relation to the Father, which has no parallel anywhere else, is the final secret of the work and ministry of Jesus.

Here are the raw materials for the highest Christology.

6. *The Kingdom involves a Cross*

Jesus began his Galilean Ministry with the announcement, 'the Reign of God has begun'. Towards its end, he said: 'The Son of man came not to be served but to serve and to give his life a ransom for many' (Mark 10.45). Since Jesus is himself both the Messenger of the Kingdom and the Son of man who must die, he poses in his own person the problem of the Kingdom and the Cross.

Half a millennium before he was born, a connexion (however adventitious) had been made between the Kingdom and the Cross. For in the fifty-second and fifty-third chapters of Isaiah, the Messenger with the good tidings has hardly done announcing, 'Your God has become King', when we read that the Servant of the Lord must suffer and die for the sins of 'the many' before he comes to his resurrection and reward. It is the career of Jesus himself, in prophecy.

It is often said that Jesus died to 'bring in' the Kingdom of God. The champions of this view declare that it must be so, if the cruciality of the Cross is to be preserved, but we

[1] For an excellent discussion of the authenticity of this saying see W. Manson, *Jesus the Messiah*, 71 ff.

have already produced irrefragable evidence that Jesus knew the Kingdom of God to be already present in his Ministry. What then? The Cross must fall *within* the Kingdom; and since, as we have already seen, the whole Ministry of Jesus, from Jordan to Calvary, is the coming of the Kingdom, the Cross must be the climacteric of his career as the Servant Messiah. It is the final act—the last and bitterest battle with the powers of evil—which crowns his work as the Servant: the condition, not of the Kingdom's coming, but of its coming 'with power'.

Men have speculated how soon Jesus foresaw the Cross as the inevitable issue of his Ministry. Some hold that he began the Ministry with brilliant hopes of success, and that only later, when these hopes faded and he saw that his enemies must infallibly kill him, he bowed to the inevitable and turned it to glorious gain. We do not read the evidence thus. On the contrary, the evidence suggests that from the time he knew himself called to be the Servant Messiah, i.e. from his Baptism, he knew the Cross to be part of his vocation. What nobody questions is that from Peter's Confession onwards he saw it as a certainty. 'The Son of man *must* suffer' (Mark 8.31), he said. It is the 'must' (*dei*) of Divine necessity: God wills the Cross for him. Hitherto he had not sought to explain Messiahship, as he understood it, to his disciples; but from the moment he does, it contains death. 'Jesus', says Goguel,[1] 'did not believe himself to be the Messiah, *although* he had to suffer. He believed himself to be the Messiah, *because* he had to suffer.'

We need not here discuss in detail Jesus' predictions of his Passion. What is plain beyond cavil is that, whenever he speaks of it, he uses the sombre language of Isa. 53. There are five such prophecies in Mark (8.31, 9.12, 9.31, 10.33 f. and 10.45). In some of them the phrasing may have been made more precise after the event; but even when we

[1] *Life of Jesus*, 392.

have eliminated all that may reasonably be credited to the influence of the Early Church, what remains is very significant. Put the 'expurgated' sentences together into one statement, and you get—a clear description of the suffering Servant of the Lord!

'[The Son of man] must suffer many things, and be rejected and set at nought, and delivered up into the hands of men, and they shall kill him. [For he came] not to be served but to serve [i.e. to be the Servant of the Lord] and to give his life a ransom for many.'[1]

(The last few words are a fairly clear translation of the Hebrew of Isa. 53.10.)

Here, then, is our problem. The Kingdom of God had, in some sense, come in the Ministry of Jesus. Yet Jesus must die as the Servant of the Lord to ransom 'the many'. The solution will appear if we spend a moment on two Kingdom sayings in St Mark.

In the first (Mark 4.11) Jesus speaks of the Kingdom as a 'mystery',[2] or secret, vouchsafed to the disciples. In the other (Mark 9.1) he declares that at no distant time men will see the Kingdom 'come with power'. The phrase 'with power' occurs also in Rom. 1.3 where the reference is to the Resurrection of Jesus. But between the coming of the Kingdom as a 'mystery' and its coming 'with power' lies the Cross. The inference is not hard to draw. The Cross was inevitable if the 'mystery' was to become an open secret. Jesus died in order that the Kingdom might come 'with power'. If further proof is needed, it is to be found in the great saying about the 'fire' and the 'baptism' (Luke 12.49 f.) whose implication is the same.

The *Te Deum* is right: it was when Jesus had 'overcome

---

[1] See R. H. Fuller, *The Mission and Achievement of Jesus*, 56.
[2] Jeremias defines the secret as 'the Kingdom's contemporary irruption in the work and words of Jesus' (*The Parables of Jesus*, 16.)

the sharpness of death' that 'he opened the Kingdom of heaven to all believers'.

7. *The Kingdom, though come, is yet to be consummated*

The phrase 'realized eschatology' does not express the whole truth about the Kingdom of God. It is not enough to say 'The Kingdom has come' when the Lord's Prayer says 'Thy kingdom come'. What did Jesus teach about the future consummation of the Kingdom of God?

Our enquiry raises a number of problems, with, on this point and that, room for difference of opinion. For one thing, there is the problem of Mark 13. Does this chapter provide, as it stands, a true picture of Jesus' thought about the future, or is it a Jewish-Christian apocalypse containing some genuine sayings of Jesus? A second difficulty, not unrelated to the first, is that sayings about the Day of the Son of man are mixed in the tradition (see, for example, the Q Apocalypse in Luke 17.22-37) with sayings in which Jesus foretells the destruction of Jerusalem. And a third is the fact that 'zero hour' parables like the Ten Virgins, the Waiting Servants, the House-breaker and the Door-keeper, which the Evangelists took to refer to the *Parousia* probably referred, on Jesus' lips, to the great crisis in the affairs of men inaugurated by his Ministry.[1]

All these things must be reckoned with when we try to reach conclusions.

I

Let us start with the sayings of Jesus which refer not to any Kingdom to come on the earth but to the eternal order of God where his Rule does not come or go but is always present. (Note: the Jews of that time thought of the Age to

[1] J. Jeremias, *The Parables of Jesus*, 36-52.

Come, or the Kingdom of God, both as an eternally existent order and as the future end of history.)[1]

Of these the two most important are:

'Many will come from the east and west and sit at table with Abraham, Isaac and Jacob in the kingdom of heaven.' (Matt. 8.11, Q. The reference to 'Abraham's bosom' in Luke 16.22 shows that the patriarchs were already believed to be in heaven.)

'I will no more drink of the fruit of the vine till that day when I drink it new [*kainos*, signifying the wine of the New Order] in the kingdom of God' (Mark 14.25).

But there are other sayings which refer to a coming of the Kingdom or of the Son of man (and the two cannot be separated) *in history*. Thus, in one place Jesus says that the Son of man will rise from the dead 'after three days', i.e. in a very short time (Mark 8.31; cf. Hos. 6.2 f.); in a second, that, at no far distant time, some will see that 'the Kingdom of God has come with power' (Mark 9.1); and in a third, that the Son of man will be seen 'coming with the clouds of heaven' (Mark 14.62; cf. Dan 7.13), i.e. will be exalted and enthroned. The thought, says Vincent Taylor,[2] is of 'entrance on a kingship which is the Father's gift. It includes all that is meant by the Resurrection, but is a more ultimate concept'.

Do these three sayings refer to different events? Much can be said for the view that they are different expressions for the same event. All three express Jesus' certainty that he is destined to triumph, and with him the cause of God which he embodies. What they assert is swift vindication after apparent defeat. Of this Jesus was quite sure.

What actually happened, we know; the Easter victory over

---

[1] See W. D. Davies, *Paul and Rabbinic Judaism*, 320. He says that the evidence he has produced delivers C. H. Dodd from the charge of 'Platonizing' levelled at him by R. Newton Flew.

[2] *Jesus and his Sacrifice*, 31.

death; the coming of the Spirit; the rise of the Apostolic Church. A new era had begun. This we may say, was the coming of Christ *in history*, and St John who tends to interpret the *Parousia* in terms of the advent of the Spirit was not wrong. As C. H. Dodd puts it:[1]

'As interpreted by Jesus himself, His total career on earth was the crisis in which the long awaited kingdom of God came upon man. The crisis began when he started his Ministry; it was complete when he returned from death. The thing had happened. They needed no longer to say, "The Son of man will come"; He had come; He was sitting on the throne of his glory, the invisible King of mankind. That is the faith of the New Testament.'

II

Did Jesus teach no more than this? No, if there was to be a coming *in history*, there was also to be another coming.

Consider, for example, these sayings, all from different Gospel sources:

The first depicts the 'revelation' of the Son of man against the background of the end of the existing order:

'As it was in the days of Noah, so it will be in the days of the Son of man. They ate, they drank, they married, they were given in marriage, until the day when Noah entered the ark and the flood came and destroyed them all. Likewise as it was in the days of Lot—they ate, they drank, they bought, they sold, they planted, they built, but on the day when Lot went out from Sodom fire and brimstone rained from heaven and destroyed them all—so it will be on the day when the Son of man is revealed.' (Luke 17.26-30 Q.).

The second saying pictures the break-down of the physical universe before the Son of man comes:

'The sun will be darkened, and the moon will not give

[1] *The Coming of Christ*, 16.

its light, and the stars will be falling from heaven, and the powers of the heavens will be shaken. And then they will see the Son of man coming in clouds with great power and glory' (Mark 13.24-26).

The third sets the scene in another world, for surely it is not in our world of space and time that the dead as well as the living will stand before the Son of man:

'When the Son of man comes in his glory, and all the angels with him, then will he sit on his glorious throne. Before him will be gathered all the nations, and he will separate them one from another as a shepherd separates the sheep from the goats' (Matt. 25.31 f. M.).[1]

Possibly these pictures owe something to the influence of the early Church's theology. Nor need we take all this tremendous imagery with prosaic literalness, since it attempts to express the unimaginable in human symbols. But, taken together, these sayings give Dominical warrant for belief in a coming of Christ *beyond* history. It is the event which we may call the consummation of the Kingdom of God:

> *Heaven and earth shall flee away*
> *When He comes to reign.*

Note:

Some have held that Jesus expected the world to end quite soon, perhaps immediately after the Resurrection. We do not read the evidence thus. If the Mustard Seed of the Kingdom is to grow into a great plant, time is obviously required. 'The Gospel must first be preached to all nations,' Jesus is reported to have said (Mark 13.10). Moreover, not only does his pattern for new life in the Kingdom of God imply the continuance of human society as we know it, but his forecasts of historical events lying beyond his death, like

---

[1] Cf. the two Q Judgment passages, Luke 10.12-15 and 11.31-32. The Judgment in which Sodom and Sheba figure must lie beyond history.

the destruction of Jerusalem, require that history shall go on. In any case, we must not dogmatize about the time when he himself confessed ignorance (Mark 13.32).

What will be the nature of this Coming which is the consummation of the Kingdom of God?

To begin with, it must mean the final triumph of God over the Kingdom of evil. 'D-day' will have become 'V-day', and God will be all in all.

Secondly, it must be the point at which time—and all in history which is pleasing to God—will be taken up into eternity. (Locate the Coming *in* the time-series, Niebuhr[1] has said, and you make the ultimate vindication of God *over* time, which is what the consummation of the Kingdom means, into a mere point *in* history.)

Thirdly, it must mean the confrontation of men by God in Christ. Here our clue is the First Coming. God has already revealed himself in a man from whom we may learn what sort of person it is with whom we shall have to do. We shall encounter the same person whose holiness, truth and love are known to us from the Gospels.

That it will mean Judgment is the teaching of Christ no less than of his apostles: not perhaps the legal proceedings on a cosmic scale which some have pictured, so much as the finalizing, in another world, of verdicts already passed in this one (and indeed passed by men on themselves). It is the teaching of Christ that the criterion will be men's response to such manifestation of God and his truth as was available to them in their day (Luke 11.31 f. Q.) and the love they have shown to all needy folk whom Christ calls his brethren (Matt. 25.31-46, M.). And we may well believe that the sign of the Cross will be over all (cf. Rom. 8.34).

But, equally, the consummation will mean the perfect fruition of life in the eternal world of God, the wiping away of all tears, the triumph of Christ and his saints. The super-

[1] *The Nature and Destiny of Man*, II, 299.

nal life will be like a feast (Mark 14.25) and comparable to
that of the angels of God (Mark 12.25). Then the promises
of the Beatitudes will come fully true: the mourners will
be comforted, the pure in heart will see God, and His
children will be at home in their Father's house (Matt. 5.4,
8.9).

3

THE RESURRECTION

THOUGH the New Testament nowhere describes the actual raising, it was the unshakable conviction of the first Christians that God raised Jesus from the dead. Is the message of the Resurrection history's most influential error or its most tremendous fact? This is the issue.

To begin with, it is not open to dispute that Jesus predicted triumph for himself and his cause. Not only did Isaiah foretell resurrection for the Servant of the Lord (53.10 ff.), but the Gospels testify that Jesus, who knew himself to be that Servant, foresaw beyond death victory and life. This conviction he expressed in various ways. Besides his 'formal' predictions of resurrection 'after three days' (Mark 8.31, 9.31, 10.34) he speaks of 'the day of the Son of man' (Luke 17.26 ff.; Matt. 24.27-39) and of his 'coming with the clouds of heaven', i.e. his enthronement (Mark 14.62) and predicts that the Kingdom of God will come 'with power' (Mark 9.1) and a new Israel will arise (Mark 14.58, John 2.18 f.). Possibly these various images describe the same event, a coming of the Reign of God defying exact description. But the main thing is clear enough: Jesus expected himself and his cause to be gloriously vindicated. Was he right? Did the Kingdom come with power? Did God raise Jesus from the dead?

I

It has often been said, with truth, that the primary evidence for the Resurrection is the existence of the Christian

Church. How did the frightened followers of a crucified Rabbi become the nucleus of a militant Church, a Church which has now endured for nineteen centuries? The New Testament attributes this astonishing change in Jesus' disciples to their conviction that God had raised their Master from the dead and that they had seen him alive and talked with him. ('There is no such thing in the New Testament as an appearance of the risen Saviour in which he merely appears.'[1] He always appears to his own, and in such a way that he enters into personal communication with them.) They may, of course, one and all, have been mistaken: we cannot prove beyond all doubt that they were right; but it must be said that, if 'probability is the guide of life', the probability is on their side. Beside the existence of the Church we may set the institution of 'the Lord's Day' (Rev. 1.10, Acts 20.7, I Cor. 16.2). Why did the early Christians, who were mostly Jews, change their sacred day (as we would say) from Saturday to Sunday? They did so, because it was on that day they believed Jesus had risen from the dead; and we may add that every Sunday, as it comes round, is a new argument for the Resurrection. Finally, we have to reckon with the New Testament writings themselves. Belief in the risen Christ fills the pages of the New Testament. Certain it is that every book in it—even the Epistle of James, for example, which never mentions it—is a resurrection document in the sense that but for belief in the Resurrection it would never have been written.

Faith in the Resurrection, then, does not depend primarily on the verdict we pass on this or that story of the risen Christ recorded in the Gospels. But this documentary evidence is important, and we must study it before we consider the significance of the Event to which it testifies.

[1] James Denney, *The Death of Christ*, 67.

II

The earliest documentary evidence occurs not in the Gospels but in I Cor. 15.3 ff. There Paul cites a piece of primitive Christian tradition (*paradosis*) which he had 'received', possibly at his conversion, more probably from the apostles during his first visit to Jerusalem after he became a Christian (i.e. about A.D. 35. See Gal. 1.18. Since in I Cor. 15.3 ff. Paul mentions by name only two apostles, Peter and James, and since these are the two he says he saw during his first visit to Jerusalem, we may surmise that he got the tradition from them. If this is so, the tradition is magnificently attested). In any case, the tradition goes back to within a very few years of the Event itself, and E. Meyer, the great German historian, rightly pronounces it 'the oldest document of the Christian Church we possess'. Independent of the Gospels, it reads like 'a guaranteed statement of the sources of evidence' used by the first preachers. We may note that it implies belief in the empty tomb, and that it records six appearances of the risen Lord (to Peter, the Twelve, five hundred brethren, James, all the apostles, and Paul himself). Two of these appearances—those to the five hundred and to James—are not referred to in the canonical Gospels. The parenthesis in v. 6, though probably no part of the tradition, is interesting; for it is Paul's way of saying to doubters: 'Most of the witnesses are still alive to be questioned'.

To this piece of tradition we may add the references to the Resurrection (of which perhaps the most interesting is that in Acts 10.40-42) contained in the Jewish-Christian *kerygma* of the Acts speeches. These, resting as they probably do on very early tradition, must be counted important.

Now we may turn to the Gospels. Many people have an uneasy feeling that the stories about the risen Christ in the Gospels, being somehow different from the stories concerning Jesus' earthly Ministry, are less worthy of credence. So far as their form goes, this is not so. C. H. Dodd,[1] after applying the methods of Form Criticism to them, concludes that in point of form they are no different from the other stories about Jesus, that they can be similarly classified, and that therefore they deserve the same consideration, not only as testimonies to the faith of the first Christians but as records of things that really happened.

We may summarize them.

Mark 16 tells how, on the first Easter morning, the women found the tomb empty, how 'a young man' told them that Jesus was risen, and how they fled in fear. Though the end of Mark has probably been lost, enough survives to show what the climax of the story was.

Matt. 28, after describing the empty tomb, records an appearance of the risen Lord to the women and an appearance to eleven disciples on a mountain in Galilee where, after giving them their 'marching orders', Jesus promises them his abiding presence. (Peculiar to Matthew are the references to the guard at the tomb, the descending angel, and the earthquake.)

Luke 24 tells how the women, after finding the tomb empty, brought the news to the incredulous Eleven. He then records three appearances: to Cleopas and another on the Emmaus Road, to Peter (Luke 24.34), and to the Eleven and others in Jerusalem before Jesus led them out 'as far as Bethany' and 'parted from them'.

John 20-21 tells how Mary Magdalene found the tomb empty, and how Peter and the Beloved Disciple (John?) visited it to verify her news. He then records four appearances: to the Magdalene in the Garden, to ten disciples the same day behind closed doors in Jerusalem, to the same ten plus Thomas in the same place a week later and to seven disciples by the Lake of Galilee.

[1] In *Studies in the Gospels* (ed. D. E. Nineham), 9-35.

How shall we judge these narratives? In Matthew we find some embroidering of the miraculous (Matt. 28.2-4) and in Luke what some think is a tendency to materialize (Luke 24.42. Cf. Luke 3.22). But, if we take them as a whole, they are not only notably free of apocalyptic features, but, for the most part, vivid, life-like and self-authenticating. When Mark tells of the women's discovery of the empty tomb, or Luke records the Walk to Emmaus, or John relates Mary Magdalene's meeting with Jesus in the Garden, we feel we are reading real history.

That all these narratives cannot be woven into a single consistent harmony hardly needs saying. We cannot be sure, for example, when and where Jesus first appeared. Was it to the women (Matt. and John)? Or was it to Peter, as I Cor. 15.5 and Luke 24.34 imply? Again, Matthew and John locate the appearances in both Jerusalem and Galilee, Luke in Jerusalem only. But these uncertainties and inconsistencies, so far from discrediting the stories, show that no harmonizing instinct has been busy on them; and discrepancies in several accounts of an event, as every student of history knows, are far from proving that an event did not occur. (Lessing once pleaded for justice in handling the Gospels. If Livy, Polybius, Dionysius and Tacitus describe the same event in discrepant ways, we do not deny that the event occurred. Why should we treat the four Evangelists differently?)

On what, then, do our accounts of the Resurrection agree? On two things:

(1) That the tomb was empty. Paul's tradition implies this. So does the apostolic preaching in Acts.[1] The four evangelists declare it. The silence of the Jews confirms it.

(2) That the Resurrection occurred 'on the third day' and that Jesus appeared to many of his followers, both men and women, on this and succeeding days.

---

[1] In the use of Ps. 16.10 (Acts 2. 27, 31).

If we are faithful to the evidence, we must start from the fact of the empty tomb. The theory that the body of Jesus was stolen or hidden is frankly incredible. Had the Romans or the Jews removed it secretly, it would have been easy to refute the Christians' claim by producing it. We may be sure that they did not, because they could not. Equally incredible, as even a Jew like Klausner admits, is the suggestion that the disciples hid his body and then went forth to declare that Jesus had risen from the dead. If then we accept the empty tomb, one of two explanations is open to us. Either we say that Jesus was resuscitated from the grave in his former body—in which case we must face the problem of what eventually happened to it after 'the forty days ', or we may agree with a long line of Christians from St. Paul to Bishop Westcott, that the physical body of our Lord was transformed in the grave into a spiritual body, a body no longer subject to the ordinary limitations of space and time. It is worth noticing here how evangelists like St Luke and St John, despite all differences, agree about the nature of the Lord's risen body. On the one hand, what they tell us suggests something quite un-earthly, since Jesus can come and go through closed doors and appear and disappear at will. On the other hand, the risen body has earthly features, since Jesus is said to have eaten and to have allowed himself to be touched. This combination of un-earthly and earthly features, the evangelists testify, characterized the reality of the Resurrection. This suggests that, in trying to fathom the mystery of the first Easter Day, we should think of something essentially other-worldly—a piece of heavenly reality—invading this world of time and sense and manifesting itself to those with ' eyes of faith '. We are concerned with an unmistakably divine event which yet occurred in this world of ours, on an April day in A.D. 30 while Pontius Pilate was Roman governor in Judea. . . .

There we may wisely leave the matter; for the chief thing in the Gospels is the disciples' invincible conviction that Jesus had survived death in the fullness of his personal life and had made his presence known to them by appearances which compelled them to say, 'We have seen the Lord'. Only on this basis can we explain the astounding change which came over the disciples, the converting power of the message they went forth to proclaim, and the experience of fellowship with a living Lord which has been the vital nerve of true Christianity for nineteen centuries.

III

What did the Resurrection mean for the first Christians? And what sort of event is postulated by the preaching of the Apostles? We cannot rest content with the vague statement that 'something happened' which persuaded them that Jesus still lived on. Any account we give must be such as to explain the theology of the Resurrection which runs through the New Testament and the Gospel of the risen Christ by which uncounted millions have lived and died.

We may start by saying that the Resurrection meant *the vindication of righteousness*. For consider: if the story of Jesus ended at the Cross, it is stark, unmitigated tragedy and, what is more, the proof that there is no spiritual rhyme or reason in the universe. Here (to put it in the lowest terms) was a Man with an unclouded vision of moral truth, a Man who not only utterly trusted God but 'hazarded all at a clap' upon his faith in him. He made the final experiment, *experimentum crucis*. If that life went out in utter darkness, there is no 'Friend behind phenomena', as he believed, but only, in Hardy's phrase, 'a vast Imbecility'. The New Testament speaks far otherwise. It declares that when Jesus laid down his life on God, Nature echoed and rang to his venture of faith. God raised him from the dead,

God vindicated his Son, and in vindicating him, vindicated his righteousness.

But in an even more specific way divine righteousness was vindicated by the Resurrection. In the Bible (the Psalms, II Isa., St Paul etc.) the 'righteousness of God' is another name for the salvation of which God is the author —it expresses the saving purpose of Him whose property it is to 'put things right' for his people. Now the Man who made the *experimentum crucis* was one who uniquely embodied that purpose of God in himself. He was the Son of man come, in God's name, to 'seek and to save the lost'. He believed that, if the 'many' were to be 'ransomed', he must lay down his life as the Servant Messiah. So, embodying in himself that purpose and making himself utterly one with sinners, Jesus went down to death. Was he deluded? On the third day, says the tradition in its oldest form (I Cor. 15.4), God raised Jesus—and all that he represented—from the grave. The Resurrection is the making manifest by miracle of the victory of God's saving purpose which took Jesus to the Cross.

Next, the Resurrection signified *the defeat of death*. This needs careful defining. Let us clarify it by saying that the first Christians did not regard the Resurrection as a dramatic verification of the truth of human survival of death: one more stone, so to speak, added to the cairn of proof of the immortality of the soul (a doctrine which in any case is Greek, not Jewish). They said that Jesus had *overcome* death, not merely survived it. They spoke of resurrection. Now resurrection, a characteristically Jewish doctrine, means various things: first, that Jesus was truly dead; second, that he lived again not merely as a disembodied spirit but in the fullness of his personality, so that, as the records say, he was, though different, still recognizably the same person; and that, above all, what had happened was incontrovertibly a great act of God. (Notice, in the New

Testament, that the writers say, 'he was raised' rather than
'he rose'.) But the Resurrection of Jesus meant even more:
it implied, as we have seen, that the cause which he embodied had also triumphed over death, that in the risen
Messiah the Reign of God had come 'with power'. In short,
the Resurrection was, for the first Christians, an eschatological act of God as new as the primal act of creation: an
act in which the strong Son of God had vanquished sin and
death and inaugurated in miracle the New Age. 'The
apostles knew that in the Resurrection of Christ another
world had come, and that they were already its citizens.'[1]

As the Resurrection meant a new mode of life for Jesus,
so it carried the promise of life for all who were his. He had
given his life to 'ransom' men from their ancient enemies,
sin and death and the devil, and in his Resurrection triumph
was victory for all who trusted in him. This is the basic
meaning of Paul's argument in I Cor. 15. If One, and that
One he who carried in his own person the whole destiny of
God's People, had shattered the myth of death's invinci-
bility, there was life in prospect for all who were his. 'As
in Adam all die, even so in Christ shall all be made alive.'
And the Power which took Jesus out of the grave was available for all his, not merely at the end of their earthly journey,
but here and now.

Lastly, the Resurrection (as the Book of Acts shows)
meant *the ongoing Ministry*.[2] During his Ministry Jesus
had described his blood-baptism as a means of initiation
into a fuller and freer activity (Luke 12.49 f.), as though
visualizing a time when he would be 'let loose in the world
where neither Roman nor Jew could stop his truth'. And so,
as a mere matter of history, it proved to be.

If we ask what precisely it was that Caiaphas, Pilate and
the rest were trying to do on the first Good Friday, the

[1] A. M. Ramsey, *The Resurrection*, 33.
[2] T. W. Manson, *The Servant Messiah*, 89.

answer is that they were trying to stop what we call the Ministry of Jesus. Now, in the story of the wonderful sequel, this or that point may be doubtful; but one thing is certain —the Ministry of Jesus was *not* stopped. On the contrary, it went on and went forward. *Vexilla Regis prodeunt!*

St Luke was right when he summarized all that led up to the Resurrection thus: ' All that Jesus *began* to do and to teach' (Acts 1.1). The Resurrection was the end of the beginning or (as the first Christians saw it) the beginning of the End. In any case, in the light of the Resurrection the Ministry of Jesus found its climax, as the Cross was to find its interpretation, and the future, its path to power and victory.

Part Two

4

THE FIRST PREACHERS
OF THE FACT

JESUS CHRIST was crucified probably in the year A.D.
30; St Paul's earliest letter cannot have been written much
before A.D. 50. These twenty years some call the 'pre-
Pauline', others 'the twilight period'. Twilight suggests
dim light; and certainly our light on this period is dimmed
through lack of contemporary documents. But dim light, as
we shall see, is not darkness. This is the period of the oral
transmission of the Gospel when hundreds of the eye-wit-
nesses of Jesus still survived, when the Gospel, as it moved
out into the wider world, changed its Aramaic dress for a
Greek one, and when little Christian congregations were
springing up in Syria and beyond it, like tiny volcanic
islands in the vast sea of paganism.

What are our sources of information? Primarily, two: the
first half of the book of Acts which tells the story of the
Primitive Church in a broadly trustworthy way; and,
second, those passages in Paul's letters which are described
as *paradosis* (i.e. 'tradition' which he 'received' from his
Christian predecessors) or which for various reasons—
stylistic, doctrinal etc.—we may confidently pronounce pre-
Pauline.

The questions to be answered are these: What was the
message of the first preachers? How did they proclaim

Christ and his work? How did they conceive of the Church and the sacraments, of the Christian way and the Christian hope?

Before we proceed, let us underscore one point. In the transition from the Synoptic Gospels to the Acts of the Apostles (which we are now making) the terms change, but the Gospel does not. The message of the earliest apostles, as we shall see, is continuous with the Gospel of Jesus—is, indeed, the same Gospel, provided we remember that between Jesus' preaching and theirs lie the Cross, the Resurrection and the Day of Pentecost. The present point, however, is terminological. In the Synoptic Gospels the Kingdom of God forms the central theme. In Acts the apostles preach now Christ, now the Kingdom (cf. Acts 8.5, 12). Paul talks of preaching Christ, never of preaching the Kingdom. (If he had announced in Corinth or in Ephesus the establishment of another Kingdom he would have found himself in a Roman gaol sooner than he did.) Are we witnessing here the process whereby a Gospel about the Kingdom was ousted by a Gospel about Christ? No, the change concerns the terminology, not the content of the Gospel. In the Synoptics the Kingdom of God is, in a 'mysterious' sense, Christ himself. Similarly, from their later vantage-point, the apostles regard the Kingdom as having come in the life, death and resurrection of Jesus and the advent of the Spirit; and to preach these events in their saving significance is to proclaim the Kingdom. If we like, we may say that before the first Easter Day the Kingdom was Christ 'in a mystery' (Mark 4.11); after the Resurrection and the coming of the Spirit, Christ—the living, ubiquitous Christ —was the disclosure, the open secret, of the Kingdom, and to accept him as Saviour was to be 'in the Kingdom', to be saved.

1. *Their Message*

In the beginning was the *kerygma*.[1] A generation before St Mark's Gospel appeared, and at least fifteen years before Paul wrote his first letter, the apostles were proclaiming their *kerygma*, or message of salvation. *Keryssō*, the Greek verb from which *kerygma* comes, means 'I proclaim'; it describes the work of a herald. And *kerygma*, usually translated 'preaching' in the AV, signifies not so much the action of the herald as what he proclaims—his message or announcement. It is a synonym for 'Gospel'.

We have two sources for its reconstruction: the speeches attributed to Peter in Acts 1-10 (notably the sermon on the day of Pentecost and the speech to Cornelius), and the 'traditional' passages in Paul (I Cor. 11.23 ff., 15.3 ff., Rom. 1.2 f., 4.25, 10.8 f., I Thess. 1.10, Phil. 2.6-11 etc.). The first source raises the question: if Luke wrote Acts fifty years later, can we trust these Petrine speeches to reproduce reliably the preaching of the earliest days? In answer the scholars tell us that, while we must not look in these speeches for the apostles' *ipsissima verba*, we may reasonably regard them as summaries of the kind of things they said. Their innocence of Pauline doctrine, their primitive Christology, and their strong Semitic colouring, all argue the presence in them of very early tradition. Aramaic sources, oral or written, probably lay at Luke's disposal.

If now we compare these speeches with Paul's 'traditional' material, the broad lines of the apostolic *kerygma* begin to emerge. The *kerygma* starts by claiming that the Old Testament promises have been fulfilled, and the New

---

[1] The classical discussion is C. H. Dodd's *The Apostolic Preaching and its Developments*. Bultmann holds that the *kerygma* of the Hellenistic Church at Antioch differed radically from the Jerusalem Church's *kerygma*. Paul was completely unaware of this difference (I Cor. 15.11), for which Bultmann produces no satisfactory evidence.

Age has come with the coming of Jesus Christ. Then it relates the high-lights of the Story of Jesus—his baptism, Ministry and mighty works, his crucifixion and death, his resurrection and exaltation to heaven—and it ends with a reference to the Holy Spirit and to the return of Christ. Then comes an appeal to men to repent and believe and be baptized.

A reporter's summary of an early Christian sermon would have read something like this:

> The prophecies are fulfilled, and the New Age has dawned.
> The Messiah, born of David's seed, has appeared.
> He is Jesus of Nazareth, God's Servant, who
>> Went about doing good and healing by God's power,
>> Was crucified according to God's purpose,
>> Was raised from the dead on the third day,
>> Is now exalted to God's right hand,
>> And will come again in glory for judgment.
> Therefore let all repent and believe and be baptized for the forgiveness of sins and the gift of the Holy Spirit.

So stated, a sermon like this would have taken only a minute or two to deliver. We must suppose that in practice the preacher would fill out this or that point as the needs of his audience required, dwelling perhaps on the argument from prophecy, or telling stories about the wonderful Ministry, or citing witnesses to the Resurrection, or pointing to the signs of the Spirit's presence, and setting forth the whole complex of events as a mighty act of God which challenged men to decision.

Two points about the *kerygma* as a whole we must underline.

The first is that *this primitive Gospel was rooted in the Gospel preached by Jesus.*

The claim that the prophecies were fulfilled corresponds

to the claim with which Jesus opened his Ministry in Galilee: 'the appointed time has fully come' (Mark 1.15).

Jesus is the Messiah, said the first preachers. Our Lord knew himself to be the Messiah (Mark 14.61 f.), even if during the Ministry he veiled his claim.[1] Likewise, as we have seen, he interpreted his Messiahship in terms of Isaiah's Servant of the Lord.

As the *kerygma* attributes Christ's mighty works to the fact that 'God was with him' (Acts 10.38), so Jesus said, 'if I by the finger of God cast out demons, then the Kingdom of God has come upon you' (Luke 11.20).

'Jesus' death accorded with God's purpose in the scriptures,' said the apostles. Jesus himself predicted his death in words from Isa. 53. 'Raised on the third day,' declared the apostles. Jesus himself foretold his victory over death in words reminiscent of Hos. 6.2.[2] 'Exalted to God's right hand' ran the apostolic testimony. 'You will see the Son of man sitting at the right hand of Power,' said Jesus before Caiaphas (Mark 14.62). 'He will come again in glory,' said the apostles. Jesus himself, as we saw, looked not only for a triumph in history but for a coming beyond it.[3]

This correspondence between the Gospel preached by Jesus and the *kerygma* of the apostles is certainly impressive. It assures us that the foundations on which the early Church built its theology were foundations in which Jesus himself had laid the chief stones.

As our first point looks back to the teaching of Jesus, so our second looks forward to the theology of the apostolic

[1] On the title 'Son of David' see Mark 10.37 f. (Bartimæus) and 12.35-37. The presumption of the evidence is that 'Jesus believed himself to be of David's house'. (V. Taylor, *St. Mark*, 491.)

[2] See *The Work and Words of Jesus*, 107.

[3] Few as they are, the Synoptic sayings about the Spirit are sufficient to prove that Jesus promised divine power and guidance to the disciples after he was gone. The Johannine teaching about the Spirit, especially the five Paraclete sayings, here supplements the scanty Synoptic data.

Church. It is this. *The pattern of the kerygma runs right through the New Testament, giving to it, amid all its diversity, a deep essential unity.* Whatever the literary form may be—Gospel, History, Epistle, Apocalypse—and whoever the writer—Luke, Paul, John, the Writer to the Hebrews—the *kerygma* can be traced in the work. St Mark's Gospel is expanded *kerygma*, as the *kerygma* controls the structure of the other three Gospels; its notes ring out clearly in the preaching of the first apostles; it throbs through the epistles of Paul and Peter and John; and it can be heard in the hieratic theology of Hebrews no less than in the apocalyptic drama of Revelation. Years ago, P. T. Forsyth[1] discerned all this when he wrote of New Testament times: 'There was no universal theological formula, there was not an orthodoxy, but there certainly was a common apostolic Gospel, a *kerygma*'.

This *kerygma* was ultimately embalmed in the Apostles' Creed.

2. *Christ and His Work*

How did the first Christians conceive of their risen Master? One chief consequence of the Resurrection was that it gave a new dimension to the person of Jesus, so that previous titles (Teacher, Prophet, etc.) became outdated and new ones had to be found. The first Christians found four: Messiah, Lord, Son of God and Servant of God. Observe that Jesus' own self-designation 'the Son of man' is not among them; indeed, outside the Gospels, it occurs but once in the New Testament (Acts 7.56). But its eclipse is understandable: not only was it too burdened with mystery for general use, but it was also quite meaningless to Gentile ears.

To begin with, let us note that the first Christians never questioned the true humanity of Jesus. 'Jesus of Nazareth

[1] *The Principle of Authority*, 141.

a man,' Peter is reported as saying on the day of Pentecost (Acts 2.22). But to describe the Risen One simply as a man was not enough. He was more—much more. What then? Let us remember that the Old Testament was the Bible of the first Christians and supplied the starting-point for all their thinking. When therefore they began to consider what place their Master held in the designs of God for men, it was to these scriptures that they turned for categories and titles to describe him.

On the title, Messiah, we need not dwell long. It is not in doubt that the first apostles 'preached Jesus as the Messiah' (Acts 5.42; cf. 2.31, 36 etc.). He was the Deliverer of Israel's centuries-old dreaming. In affirming him to be the Messiah, the apostles were endorsing a claim that Jesus had himself made. Conceptions of the Messiah in contemporary Judaism varied greatly; yet underlying them all was the idea that the Messiah was the Divinely-appointed Head of the People of God and the Bearer of his Rule to men. This person, then, they claimed, was no longer a pious hope but a blessed reality. He was the man once known as Jesus of Nazareth whom God had raised from the dead. To be sure, he bore little resemblance to the Messiah of orthodox dreaming: it might even be said that, though Jesus had clothed himself in the images of Messianic promise, he had, in living them out, literally *crucified* them; but of his true claim to the title, after the Resurrection, his followers had no doubt. This title defined their Master's relation to the age-old hope of Israel. He was its fulfilment.[1]

---

[1] When Christians took to calling Jesus Lord instead of Messiah, the Liberals, wrongly, supposed that they were 'heightening the Christology'. The point is that Jewish Messianism does not yield a Christology of *status* in metaphysical terms—it yields a Christology of *function* in terms of history. But the function of the Messiah is undoubtedly a *divine* function, viz., his inauguration of God's Kingdom. The Messiah's action in history *is* God's own action. G. Dix, *Jew and Greek*, 79.

Messiah, in its Greek form 'Christ', soon became a proper name. The other title Peter is said to have given Jesus on the day of Pentecost, 'Lord' (Acts 2.36), had a greater future before it.

The Greek word for 'Lord' is *Kyrios* (Aramaic, *Mar*). Now, in the Greek Old Testament (the Bible of the early Church) *Kyrios* renders not only *Adonai* but the ineffable name of God (Yahweh). Here, then, was a title that could be charged with supreme religious meaning. Can we believe that the first Christians so styled Jesus?

Bousset said No.[1] *Kyrios*, he argued, was a title commonly given to cult-deities in the Greek Mystery religions, as it was given honorifically to Roman emperors. The contemporary pagan world knew 'Lords many' (I Cor. 8.5). Therefore we must not suppose that Aramaic-speaking Christians ever called Jesus 'Lord'. Not till Christianity moved out into the Greco-Roman world did men worship him as 'Lord'.

But the facts are firmly against Bousset. The phrase 'at the right hand of God', derived from Psalm 110.1, was a fundamental text of the primitive *kerygma*; and this doctrine of Christ's session at God's right hand certainly implies the Lordship of Christ.[2] But, as if to prove conclusively that the first Christians worshipped Jesus as Lord, Paul has preserved for us the Aramaic-speaking Church's prayer, '*Marana tha!* Our Lord, come!' (I Cor. 16.22), an invocation certainly addressed to Jesus. This said, we may readily admit that, when the Gospel became Hellenized, the title 'Lord' naturally won a much wider currency.

'Lord', in this exalted sense, is a post-Resurrection title. It defines Jesus in relation to the worshipping community.

[1] In his book *Kyrios Christos*.

[2] For an interesting and, in my view, cogent suggestion that Jesus himself supplied the raw materials for this confession of his Lordship, see R. H. Fuller, *The Mission and Achievement of Jesus*, 112-114.

He is its Lord to whom veneration is due. Indeed, we can hardly overrate the importance of the title. To invoke Jesus as Lord is tantamount to praying to him (as the dying Stephen is said to have done); to confess him as Lord is next door to worshipping him. Rightly does Vincent Taylor say:[1] 'Implicit in the recognition of the Lordship of Jesus is the acknowledgment of his essential divinity.'

Did the earliest Christians think of Jesus as God's Son? If our only source were the early speeches in Acts, the answer would have to be No. But some twenty years later Paul calls Jesus God's Son, as though the title were his without dispute; and in two passages commonly allowed to be pre-Pauline, I Thess. 1.10 and Rom. 1.3 f.,[2] the words 'his Son' occur. These passages push the title back to at least A.D. 40 and probably earlier. When, therefore, we find so sceptical a critic as Rudolf Bultmann[3] freely admitting that the Aramaic-speaking Jerusalem Church named Jesus 'the Son of God', we might think the question settled. But, says Bultmann, when these Jerusalem Christians so named Jesus, they were using the title in a Messianic sense; and their usage derived from the Messianic interpretation of Ps. 2.7. Thus he refuses the far more probable explanation—that Jesus was known to have so styled himself, and that not merely in a Messianic way, but in a sense claiming unique Sonhood to God (Mark 13.32. Cf. Mark 12.6, Matt. 11.27, Luke 10.22. Cf. also Jesus' use of the word *Abba*.). Corroboration is to be found in the common early Christian description of God as 'the God and Father of our Lord Jesus Christ'.

'Lord,' however, seems to have been the commoner title

---

[1] *The Names of Jesus*, 51.

[2] See Dibelius on I Thess 1.10 (*Handbuch zum Neuen Testament*) and Dodd on Rom. 1.3 f. (*Moffatt New Testament Commentary*).

[3] *Theology of the New Testament*, 28, 32.

of Jesus; and if we ask why, the probable answer is that, while the first Christians called Jesus God's ' Son,' the word belonged to teaching rather than to worship. While they believed in 'the Son' (cf. the D. text in Acts 8.37 which may be original),[1] they confessed him as 'Lord'.

The title 'Son of God' describes Jesus' relation to the unseen Father. It points to the deepest secret of his being, suggesting one aware that he comes to men from the depths of the being of God.

If the first Christians saw in Jesus the Messiah, worshipped him as Lord, and believed in him as the Son of God, they employed yet another title to set forth his saving significance. They called him 'the Servant of God', the Servant of Isaiah's great prophecies.

Like most things in the New Testament, this has been disputed, but on the flimsiest of grounds,[2] for the case is cumulative and strong:

First, we have seen that Jesus believed himself to be the Servant Messiah (Part I); and we can hardly believe that his first followers, who preserved sayings like Mark 10.45, completely forgot this.

Second, and as if to confirm our first point, we find Peter four times in the early chapters of Acts (3.13, 26, 4.27, 30) calling Jesus 'God's Servant' (*pais theou*). A little later, Philip expressly tells the Ethiopian Eunuch that Jesus is the fulfilment of Isa. 53 (Acts 8.26-40).

Third, two passages commonly adjudged pre-Pauline[3]

[1] 'I believe that Jesus Christ is the Son of God'. Lake and Jackson call this 'perhaps the earliest form of baptismal creed'. Cullmann, who believes the reading original, says, 'This short confession refers to earliest times.'

[2] e.g. that the Greek phrase *pais theou* comes from the LXX, must therefore have been first used by Greek-speaking Christians, and cannot go back to the Aramaic-speaking Mother Church. The weakness of this argument appears in the fact that the LXX also uses *doulos* in translating Isaiah's *ebed*.

[3] Even by Bultmann, *op. cit.*, 82, 125.

(Rom. 4.25 and Phil. 2.6-11) describe Jesus' saving work in words from Isa. 53.

We need not therefore hesitate to follow Jeremias[1] in tracing this title back to 'the oldest Palestinian Church'. Meantime, enough has emerged to show how wrong it is to suppose that theology is a late addendum to Christianity, the elaborate mystification by later intellectuals of something originally quite simple, experimental and untheological. As far back as we can go into Christian origins, we find a doctrine of Christ. The momentous word of Nicea may still be a long way off, but already in the men of this 'twilight period' we find perceptions of the true rank of Jesus, as the Christian Church has understood it all down the centuries.

We turn now to the work of Christ.

As everybody knows, St Paul found in the Cross the heart of the Gospel, so that he called it 'the Word of the Cross'. But the days are past in which Paul could be given the credit—or blame—for this discovery. That the Cross was central in the earliest Church is proved by a three-fold chain of evidence.

To begin with, we learn from St Paul how his Christian predecessors viewed the Cross. It was part of the Christian *credo* which he received soon after his conversion (i.e. within a few years of the crucifixion) that 'Christ died for our sins according to the scriptures' (I Cor. 15.3). A few verses later Paul declares that this was the common apostolic Gospel. We infer that there was no Gospel known in the primitive Church which did not, in Paul's phrase, 'placard' Christ as crucified for men's sins.

The second link in the chain is supplied by the *kerygma* in Acts. We have already cited the references to Jesus as 'God's Servant' with all which the title implies. Here we may add two fresh pieces of evidence. In Acts 2.23 Peter

[1] *The Servant of God.*

declares that Christ was 'delivered up according to the definite plan and foreknowledge of God'. Clearly the earliest preachers saw Christ's death as an integral part of God's design for man's salvation. Nor is this all. Twice in Acts (5.30 and 10.39) Jesus' death is significantly called 'hanging on a tree'. This phrase points us back to the Jewish belief that a man 'hanged on a tree' was a man 'accursed by God' (Deut. 21.22 f.). Anyone who so described Christ's death had not only seen the 'scandal' of the Cross but had somehow divined that he bore the curse for others.

The final link is found in the Synoptic Gospels. The Church preserved two sayings of Jesus in which he gave a redemptive meaning to his death—the Ransom Saying (Mark 10.45) and the Word over the Cup (Mark 14.24). Since both these sayings owe their preservation to the memory of the Twelve, they must stem from the original Jerusalem tradition.

Only one conclusion seems admissible: 'the Word of the Cross' lay at the heart of the earliest Gospel.

We cannot say how soon the Christians reached this understanding. At first, perhaps, like the two disciples on the Road to Emmaus, they saw the Resurrection as the incredible reversal of unmitigated tragedy. Then slowly, gradually, as they pondered the fact, what had seemed only the crime of cruel men became the glorious deed of God; and seeking a clue, they remembered their Master's predictions of his passion, were led to the prophecy of Isaiah as the solution of the mystery, and summed it up by saying: 'Christ died for our sins according to the scriptures'.

It may be hard to say how far they held a doctrine of the Atonement. But if, starting from Isa. 53, they 'preached the good news about Jesus', as Philip did, must we not credit them with some understanding of the profound soteriology of that chapter? Now the doctrine there is one of representative suffering for the sins of 'the many', with the idea of substitution well in the foreground. It is no rash guess that the earliest preachers saw in Jesus the great Sin-bearer by whose stripes they were healed.

3. *The Holy Spirit*

We have been considering how the earliest Christians conceived of the work of Christ. But was not that work done, and had not Christ returned to the unseen world? And must not the whole Fact of Christ have tended henceforth to recede, month by month, and year by year, into the unreturning past? What actually happened seems to have been the exact opposite. 'No apostle ever *remembered* Christ,' it has been said. Instead, they dwelt not on the past but on the present, and they faced the future with glowing hope. What made this transforming difference? The event of Pentecost, says the record in Acts. Their Lord might be exalted to heaven, but he was still with them, through the Spirit; and the ends for which he had lived and died were now being secured by this strange new power at work in their midst.

It has been observed that, if St Luke had not given us the narrative of Acts 2, we should have been under the necessity of conjecturing such an event. True, Luke's reference to the polyglot endowment of the apostles at Pentcost staggers belief: and we may well find the true miracle not in some apostolic aptitude for foreign tongues but in their ability to testify with tongues of fire to Christ's resurrection and Lordship. But, explain Acts 2 as we will, none but the most sceptical will deny its basic truth—that on a definite day the followers of Jesus received a monumental access of new power which they identified with the promised Spirit of God, and which not only wonderfully vivified the Fact of Christ but invaded all their life and worship.

But can we accept these early chapters in Acts as evidence for the earliest Christian beliefs about the Holy Spirit? Are they not a reading back into the narrative of later doctrines? For a first point, we may say without fear of contradiction that the apostle Paul certainly did not originate belief in the Holy Spirit, that it was there in the Church before he came on the scene. For a second point, if we except Luke's 'mistake' about the true nature of the 'tongues', there is nothing in what he says about the Spirit alien to what we otherwise know about the earliest days, and much that is entirely credible. The whole conception of the Spirit is Hebraic rather than Hellenic, and we find no trace of Paul's developed doctrine of the Holy Spirit as we find it, say, in Romans 8. What we find in these early chapters of Acts is men suddenly aware of a new power let loose in the world and in themselves, and tending, understandably enough, to attribute all abnormal phenomena to it. To the illapse of the Spirit are ascribed speaking with tongues, the shaking of the house where the apostles were gathered, and the 'rapture' of Philip, and the concomitants of the Spirit are 'power', 'joy' and 'faith'. The language used is that of experimental religion, and the Spirit is a gift of power rather than a personal presence: a gift indeed of God (2.38, 8.20 etc.) mediated by the exalted Christ (2.33), in fulfilment of prophecy (2.16 f.). Its sphere of operation is the Church, and somehow (the evidence is a little conflicting) it is linked with baptism, whether as pre-condition or consequence. The day will come when Paul, building on all this experience, will speak of 'the Spirit of Christ', will ethicize its workings, and will present Christianity as a religion of the Spirit; but as yet the Spirit means power—new, God-given power, helping the apostles to testify to Christ, expressing itself in tongues and prophecy (inspired preaching), enabling them to work miracles, and reinforcing the victorious faith and 'glad fearlessness' (*parrhēsia*) of men like Peter, Stephen and Barnabas. But the main point is that the Holy Spirit is an experience inseparably connected with Christ, as it is a token that he is present in their midst, empowering them for their missionary task.

4. *Church and Sacraments*

The fellowship of the Holy Spirit was the Church. Men sometimes picture the first Christians as a band of bewildered Galileans huddled together for mutual encouragement, one among several Jewish sects and quite unaware of being anything more. Then gradually *esprit de corps* and persecution closed their ranks, giving them an adventitious unity which, three or four decades later, developed into the one *Ecclēsia* of the Epistle to the Ephesians.

The picture in Acts may be idealized in places, but this is not the impression it leaves on us. At first, the Christians do not break with Judaism; contact with Temple and synagogue continues; and when Peter speaks, it is as an Israelite to the men of Israel. And yet from the beginning they held one belief which marked them out from their fellow-Jews— the belief that the Messiah had come. More, they had received the gift of the Holy Spirit promised for the last days. Dimly, then (for life ever precedes doctrine) they must have felt their distinctiveness. They were conscious of being the new Israel which had served itself heir to the promises made to the fathers (Acts 3.25 f.). At first, they felt no need to define their attitude to such things as the Law and circumcision; but when the Hellenist Stephen, true precursor of Paul, had said his say and paid with his life for it, this issue was sharply posed and was to vex the Church for many a day.

St Luke has summarized the life of the earliest Christian community thus:

'They devoted themselves to the apostles' teaching and

fellowship, to the breaking of bread and the prayers' (Acts 2.42).

'Fellowship' represents the Greek *koinōnia*, whose root meaning is 'sharing', and probably what St Luke means here is brotherly love in action. This seems confirmed by the statement that 'they had all things in common'. To call this Communism is misleading—it is simply a practical sharing of property on the basis of love. This love and an 'exuberant joy' (*agalliasis*: Acts 2.46) were the spiritual marks of the earliest Church which had as yet no hard-and-fast organization but was a fellowship of the Spirit in which the original apostles held the leading places.

We are to imagine, then, a little community confessing Jesus as Messiah and Lord, vividly aware of an 'upsurge of new life', living together like a big family, devoting themselves to preaching the Word, celebrating their rite of table-fellowship with their living Lord, and looking for his advent in glory.

We do not know when they first called themselves 'the *Ecclēsia*'. Perhaps it was when the first predominantly Gentile congregation arose at Antioch; but the idea behind the word was theirs from the first. *Ecclēsia*, in secular Greek, signified a popular assembly (see Acts 19.32, 39, 41). But a Greek of those days, hearing the Christians call themselves 'the *Ecclēsia*', would have been puzzled by the definite article and the odd nuance of the noun. Had he taken to reading the Greek Old Testament, his mystification would have vanished. For in the LXX *ecclēsia* commonly renders the Hebrew *Qahal*, the usual term for Israel as the gathered People of God. Thus, its adoption by the Christians expressed their claim to be the true People of God, at once old and new.

It is, of course, the Jerusalem Church which is called the *Ecclēsia* in the early chapters of Acts (e.g. Acts 5.11). But the local connexion is not the primary thing, for in Acts 9.31

we hear of 'the *Ecclēsia* throughout all Judea and Galilee and Samaria'. In other words, the *Ecclēsia* was originally domiciled in Jerusalem; but, with the spread of the Gospel, the idea arose of the local *Ecclēsia* as a microcosm, or outcrop, of the one *Ecclēsia*.

The Head of this *Ecclēsia* was the Lord Jesus, in whose name they baptized and the confession of whose Lordship —probably at baptism—made up the earliest Christian confession (Rom. 10.9, I Cor. 12.3, Phil. 2.11); and the new People of God felt that they had a mission which (assuming Stephen's speech to be broadly authentic, as it probably is) looked far beyond the bounds of Jewry.

There is nothing older in Christianity than the sacraments. Paul did not originate them; they were there from the start. The question is, What was their significance?

While the origins of Christian baptism are veiled in obscurity, we may reasonably believe that the rite was first practised in obedience to a command of the Risen Lord; for even if Matt. 28.19 is the liturgical formulation of the later Church, it testifies to their belief that such a command had been given. Christian baptism, which was the door of entry into the Church, probably dates back to the Day of Pentecost (Acts 2.38). Administered 'into Christ', or 'in the name of Christ', it signified that the baptized person passed into his possession. The mode was immersion, and baptism normally coincided with the reception of the Holy Spirit.

Probably the Baptism of Jesus supplied the type for Christian Baptism. For others, baptism with water and baptism with the Spirit could mean very different things, but in the case of Jesus the two had coincided, and henceforth their coincidence became the rule in the Church. (Cf. John 3.5. 'Except a man be born of water and the Spirit . . .') Can we say anything more about this earliest Baptism?

The Lord had described his death as a 'ransom' which

would deliver 'the many' (Mark 10.45). This representative death he had also called a 'baptism' (Luke 12.50, Mark 10.38), i.e. a religious act of cleansing undertaken not for himself but for 'the many'. May we not then say that Jesus believed that this baptism of blood would avail to cleanse the 'many' from sin? On the Day of Pentecost, when the Holy Spirit came on his followers, making the Fact of Christ real as never before, the virtue of Christ's baptism of blood became available for all, so that those who, by faith and baptism, were joined to their Lord, shared in the virtue of his atoning work. Is this all mere speculation? Apparently not, for later Christ's Baptism (i.e. of blood, on Calvary) became an important soteriological category in the New Testament. Not only so, but writing some twenty-five years after the Crucifixion to Christians in Rome he had never visited, St Paul speaks of baptism as a sacrament in which men died with Christ to sin and rose into 'newness of life' (Rom. 6.3 f.). 'Do you not know?' he writes, as though appealing to something familiar to the Church at large. Is it not likely that in the pre-Pauline Church men thought of the rite as a sacrament of union with Christ in his dying and rising?

In his picture of the Primitive Church St Luke twice refers to their 'breaking of the bread'. (Acts 2.42, 46). We naturally assume that by this he means the meal later known as 'the Lord's Supper', which in turn looked back to the Last Supper. No doubt this Supper was part of an actual common meal; but to suppose that 'the breaking of the bread' means no more than 'taking food' seems improbable. Certainly when St Paul spoke of 'the bread which we break', he meant the Lord's Supper, and in Acts not only does the stress on the 'breaking' focus the central significance of the meal, but the linkage of the bread-breaking with 'the prayers' seems to imply something more than an ordinary meal.

If, then, Luke's 'breaking of the bread' is the Eucharist, can we form any idea of how they thought about it? Twenty years later Paul interprets the Lord's Supper as a sacramental means of sharing in Christ's death (I Cor. 10.16 f.); in so doing he not only uses the phrase 'the cup of blessing' which the primitive Christians had taken over from the Jewish Church, but writes a sentence which has all the rhythm of a liturgical formula, and states his doctrine as though it were something axiomatic. Must we not conclude that he was not the first so to think of the Supper? But communion with Christ crucified was certainly not the only motif of the earliest Christian Eucharist. Luke's mention of the 'exuberant joy' of the first Christians suggests that the Easter note was not muted by the remembrance of 'the night on which he was delivered up'; and the primitive Christian *Marana tha* was probably not only a prayer for the *Parousia* but an *epiclēsis* invoking the presence of the Risen Lord at his Table. (Cf. Rev. 3.20, which has probably also a Eucharistic reference. As in the days after the first Easter in Jerusalem, so in Asia Minor later the Risen Lord was conceived to be present at the Supper.) Finally, we know that the earliest Lord's Supper had a forward-looking note. As they communed with their Risen Lord, unseen but not unknown, their thoughts leapt forward to the time when he would come in glory (I Cor. 11.26, 16.22).

Note: Some modern scholars, e.g. Lietzmann, have held that early Christianity knew two distinctive types of Eucharist: (1) a pre-Pauline Eucharist unconnected with the Last Supper and continuing the table-fellowship between Jesus and his disciples in the days of his flesh; and (2) a Lord's Supper, as in I Cor. 11, which took its origin from the Last Supper. Paul (they think) following a revelation from the Risen Lord—this is what 'I received of the Lord' means—first connected the Church's Lord's Supper with the Last Supper.

We reject this view: (1) It rest on an unlikely interpretation of 'I received of the Lord'; (2) it contradicts the contention of the Form Critics that the narratives of the Last Supper were preserved because they described the institution of the Church's sacrament; and (3) it is hard to believe that Paul could have successfully foisted on the Church at large an interpretation of the Supper which his critics would have at once branded as a daring innovation.

5. *Christian Way and Christian Hope*

Let us turn now from worship to morals.

One of the earliest names for the Christians was 'the Way' (Acts 9.2); and, whatever else it connoted, it meant that they were known to be committed to a new way of life. Did then the apostles lay down some kind of moral code for their converts, some pattern for Christian behaviour? Paul certainly did—see I Thess. 4.1 and II Thess. 3.6, and note the reference in Rom. 6.17 to a 'pattern of teaching' which was 'traditional'—and we may be quite sure he was not the first to do it. What moral tradition was this? It is now generally agreed that the ethical portions of the Apostolic letters[1] (e.g. I Thess. 4.1-12, 5.12-22, Gal. 5.13-6.10, Col. 3.1-4-6 and similar sections in I Peter, Hebrews, etc.) preserve some of it. Much of it is 'elementary ethics' with nothing distinctively Christian about it, as some is demonstrably pre-Christian. Exhortations to make a clean break with the old life; injunctions to honesty, purity, truthfulness, sober living and hard work; regulations about decent family life—this was the staple of it. The need for such elementary ethics we may understand, if we remember the pagan background of many of the converts; but might we not have expected the first Christians to seek their pattern for life in the teaching of Jesus himself?

[1] What C. H. Dodd and others call *didachē* (moral instruction).

Once again, we may argue back from Paul's practice to that of his predecessors. It was his custom when faced with hard problems of everyday conduct, to settle them with a word of the Lord, if he knew one. I Cor. 7.10 is an example. Moreover, if we study the ethical sections of his letters—particularly Rom. 12.14—we find them full of sayings of Jesus, or echoes of them. Perhaps he had a written collection of them; more probably he was drawing on an oral tradition. This brings us to the crux of the problem. If the first Christians turned to 'the Lord' for moral guidance, where do we find evidence for it?

The answer is very simple: in the Synoptic tradition of Jesus' sayings. If the Form Critics have taught us anything, it is that these Gospels are sources not only for the teaching of Jesus but for the teaching of the earliest Church. In other words, many sayings of Jesus have come down to us simply because they supplied Dominical answers to urgent ethical questions in the earliest days.

Some of them concerned such matters as sabbath-observance, ritual washing, divorce and tax-paying. It is no accident that the Synoptic Gospels preserve utterances of Jesus on such issues. These 'pronouncement stories' (as Vincent Taylor calls them) were preserved because they recorded the mind of Christ on these vexed questions. The first Christians asked: What is to be our attitude to the Jewish sabbath? Guidance was found in such Dominical pronouncements as Mark 2.23 ff., 3.1 ff., and Luke 13.10-17. What should a Christian think about the worth of ritual washings? Answer: The Lord has given us guidance about the nature of true defilement (Mark 7.1 ff.). Shall we pay taxes to Rome? Answer: the Lord has bidden us 'render unto Caesar the things that are Caesar's, and to God the things that are God's' (Mark 12.13-17). May a Christian divorce his wife? No, for the Lord has forbidden it (Mark 10.1-12). And so on.

But the first Christians needed more than pronouncements; they needed also principles for Christian action generally. This need was met by recalling the systematic teaching about life in the Kingdom which Jesus had given his disciples. Here we think primarily of what is called 'the Sermon on the Mount' (Matt. 5.7, Luke 6.20-49). This, the fruit of many teaching-sessions with his disciples, made up a Dominical pattern for life, and was undoubtedly so used from the beginning (though, of course, Matthew's present arrangement of it is later). That these sayings have been so well preserved is partly due to the fact that Jesus cast his teaching in poetical, and therefore memorable, form. But its excellent preservation is itself proof that the Primitive Church took this teaching seriously. When therefore we ask what the phrase 'the Way' meant ethically, a large part of the answer must be in terms of the teaching of the Sermon and of similar passages elsewhere in the Gospels. 'The Beatitudes of the Great Sermon, the condition of childlikeness, the forgiveness of enemies, the love which is like the love of God himself—all these go to the interpretation of that phrase the Way of the Lord'.[1]

The hope which sustained these earliest pilgrims on the Way is epitomized in two Aramaic words: '*Marana tha!* Our Lord, come!' (I Cor. 16.22). Yet we must get these words in their right perspective. It is often supposed that the article *par excellence* in the first Christian *Credo* was the Second Advent. Although the Acts *kerygma* refers only twice (Acts 3.20 f. and 10.42) to this royal Coming of Christ, there can be no question that the first Christians 'spoke to each other softly of a Hope'. But their emphasis on things was rather different. If they prayed, 'Our Lord, come!' it was because they first confessed, 'Jesus is Lord'. They believed in a final triumph of Christ because they believed in the victory already won by him. They expected cosmic

[1] R. N. Flew, *Jesus and His Church*, 159.

confirmation of Christ's victory because they held inexpugnably to his present Lordship. The *Parousia*, when it came, would be the unveiling in glory of all implied in the First Easter, and in that day Christ would be the Judge of both the quick and the dead (Acts 10.42). Then would be realized that perfect order of things of which God had spoken to his People through the prophets (Acts 3.21; cf. Īsa. 65.17-25). Meantime (in words commonly considered pre-Pauline) men were bidden 'turn to God from idols, to serve a living and true God, and to wait for his Son from heaven, whom he raised from the dead, Jesus who delivers us from the wrath to come' (I Thess. 1.9 f.).

But what gave substance to the whole Christian Hope was the Resurrection of the Lord. One Man had 'left a gaping tomb in the wide graveyard of the world', the Man who carried in his own person the destinies of God's People. As he was risen and exalted to high heaven, in his immortal life his faithful followers would surely share.

Part Three

THE INTERPRETERS OF THE FACT

5

ST PAUL

WE have been feeling our way forward amid the half-lights of the 'thirties' and the 'forties'. But with the 'fifties' daylight, in the shape of contemporary documents, is upon us. These documents are ten letters[1] of St Paul, who not only played a heroic part in the advance of the Gospel but proved himself the greatest of its early interpreters.

St Paul had two 'tutors unto Christ': one Jewish and the other Greek.

His debt to Judaism is so plain on every page that one is left wondering how scholars like Reitzenstein ever succeeded in convincing any that Paul was a thorough-going Hellenist. True, he learned his Judaism in a Hellenistic milieu; but the burden of proof lies on all who maintain that Hellenistic Judaism of the kind Paul knew differed radically from its Palestinian variety.

'A Hebrew of the Hebrews,' is Paul's own comment on

---

[1] We accept Ephesians as Paul's, but exclude the Pastorals. They probably contain, as P. N. Harrison has argued, genuine Pauline fragments; but in their present form they are the work of a Paulinist.

his spiritual pedigree (Phil. 3.5). Theologically speaking, this meant that he was reared in the *credo* of the devout Jew of his time, viz., belief in the one God righteous and holy, in the election of Israel to be his Special People, in the Law as the unique revelation of God's will for men, and in the hope of the Messiah. His letters show that, even when he became a Christian, these things remained basic to his thinking. Even if his letters and the Acts had not expressly told us that he belonged to the sect of the Pharisees and had received a rabbinical training, we should infer this from his theology. Nor let us despise these ultra-Jewish origins. 'If God was not moving in the rabbinic thought of Christ's day, what reason have we to say that he moves in the thought of to-day?'[1] In any case, the proof is everywhere in Paul. His antithesis of the spirit and the flesh stems from the Jewish doctrine of the two Impulses. His favourite phrase 'in Christ' we can understand only in terms of the Hebrew conception of corporate personality. Would any but 'a Hebrew of the Hebrews' have called Jesus 'the Last Adam' or thought of him as the new *Torah*? When Paul discusses the Christian Hope, it is the resurrection of the body, not the immortality of the soul, which concerns him. And when he dwells on the last end of God's purpose in history for Jew and Gentile, he says, very characteristically, 'And so all *Israel* shall be saved'.

What did he owe to Hellenism? He read his scriptures in a Greek translation—the Septuagint. He wrote his letters in *koinē* Greek. He spent most of his thirty years as a missionary in lands where Greek civilization met him at every turn. Twice or thrice he quotes the Greek poets; he is fond of metaphors from the Greek games; here and there he employs a Stoic word or phrase; and occasionally he uses, though often with a different meaning, terms current among the devotees of the Greek Mystery religions. But the idea

[1] P. T. Forsyth.

that he was a zealous student of Greek letters, or was deeply influenced by Stoic philosophy, is not to be taken seriously, and the theory that his theology was radically infected by the Mysteries has completely lost caste in the world of scholarship. 'St Paul', wrote Gregory Dix,[1] 'has by now stood his trial on the charge of "Hellenizing" Christianity to make it acceptable to the Greeks—and the verdict is decisively, "Not Guilty". Perhaps in a few years' time he will be charged with Rabbinizing a Galilean Gospel and making it unintelligible to Greeks! Paul, however, had many trials and usually succeeded in coming through them tolerably well.'

What of Paul's debt to those who were 'in Christ' before him, like Ananias, Andronicus and Junias (Rom. 16.7), not to mention the members of the Mother Church? Our previous studies in 'the Twilight Period' have made it abundantly clear how many stones in the great edifice of what we call 'Paulinism' were hewn into rough shape before the 'master-builder' arrived to take them over. In plain terms, a great deal of 'Paulinism' is common, apostolic Christianity, and Paul was profoundly indebted to his Christian predecessors. Here therefore we will content ourselves with listing seven of these debts: (1) The Apostolic *kerygma*; (2) the conception of Jesus as Messiah, Lord and Son of God; (3) the doctrine of the Holy Spirit as the Divine dynamic of the new life; (4) the doctrine of the Church as the new Israel; (5) the sacraments of Baptism and the Lord's Supper; (6) the 'Words of the Lord' which he quotes; and (7) the belief in Christ's *Parousia*.

One further item in these spiritual prolegomena needs to be mentioned: the influence of his conversion. It has been well said that Paul's theology bears not so much the grammarian's as the sinner's touch. It is the theology of a converted man, of one who could say, 'By the grace of God I

[1] *Jew and Greek*, 3.

am what I am '. No doubt it took time for all the implications of the Damascus Road experience to become plain to him; but we may fairly say that it brought with it three decisive consequences for his thinking. To begin with, it meant that Christ was incontrovertibly alive—alive by the power of God who by the Resurrection had set his seal on the deed of the Cross. Secondly, the Cross itself, which had been for Saul the Pharisee the place of God's curse, became for him the place of revelation—the revelation of the love of God. And, lastly, Paul knew now that ' salvation is of the Lord ', that it begins on the Divine side with an act of pure grace which man has done nothing to deserve. Small wonder that grace—the extravagant goodness of God to undeserving men—is written all over his Gospel.

CHRISTIANITY ACCORDING TO ST PAUL

The Gospel of Christ, as Paul understood it, is the Good News of the salvation which God has provided for sinners through Christ's Incarnation, Death, Resurrection and living power, and now offers to all who will believe. What we call his theology is that Gospel as explicated in his letters. It is not something we can separate from his Gospel; it is his Gospel as his mind grasped it.

In this definition of Paul's Gospel we have deliberately used the word 'salvation' to sum it up. Traditional Protestantism, following Luther, has found the heart of Paul's Gospel in the phrase ' justification by faith '. A true insight guided them in this, as we shall see. But it is wrong to say that this doctrine epitomizes Paul's Gospel. For justification by faith is only the fragment of a larger whole—the first stage on the Christian road, not the whole journey. More recently others have summed up Paul's Gospel as ' communion with Christ '. Once again, this is but an element, though a very important one, in Paul's Christianity. We need a more comprehensive word to express the richness and range of Christianity according to St Paul; and the best word at our disposal is 'salvation' (*sōtēria*).

The fundamental question for religion is the Philippian gaoler's: 'What must I do to be saved?' Paul's religion starts from this question, and he finds the answer in what he calls 'the gospel of your salvation' (Eph. 1.13). When he preached in Pisidian Antioch or wrote to the Christians in Rome, this was the word he used (Acts 13.26, Rom. 1.16).

The word 'salvation' signified well-being in all its forms, from soundness of body to the highest ideal of spiritual health. And salvation was, in a sense, what all serious-minded men in Paul's day, Gentiles no less than Jews, were seeking. For the Jew, salvation would mean primarily deliverance from the sin which separates from a holy God. For the Gentile, it would mean deliverance from all 'the slings and arrows of outrageous fortune', from Fate, fear of death and all the nameless insecurity on which we mortals hold the lease of life. But, however they construed the word, *sōtēria* was what both sought; and in the Gospel Paul claimed he had the answer to their longings, an answer in terms of the love of God to men revealed in the Cross of Jesus Christ. Nor was the Gospel, in Paul's view, a mere remedial system—something negative—security from the long-term consequences of sin or from the haunting fear of annihilation. It included not only what a man must be saved *from* but also what he must be saved *to*—reconciliation and righteousness and life.

When St Paul thought about Christian salvation, he saw it as a word with three tenses. It meant a past event, a present experience, and a future hope. 'We were saved,' he says in one place (Rom. 8.24). 'We are being saved,' he says in another (I Cor. 15.2). And 'we shall be saved', he says in a third (Rom. 5.9). Indeed, Rom. 5.1 takes in all three tenses: 'Therefore being justified by faith, we have peace with God through our Lord Jesus Christ, through whom also we have obtained access into this grace in which we stand, and rejoice in hope of the glory of God'.

I

Salvation as a past event rests on 'the finished work' of Christ—what he did for men on the Cross—and looks back to the time when the sinner, by the decision of faith, made that deliverance his own.

The thing from which we need saving is sin, indwelling sin, that radical and corporate wrongness which separates us from God and in which every son of Adam shares: 'All have sinned' (Rom. 3.23). It is no mere incident, without antecedents or consequents, but a universal state—nay, in Paul's view, a positive and destructive principle or power, endemic in man and enslaving him: 'sold under sin', we have become its slaves (Rom. 6.17, 7.14). Sin finds its 'base of operations' in 'the flesh', our fallen human nature, which gives sin its material to work on. Sin is exposed by the Law —'through the Law comes knowledge of sin' (Rom. 3.20) —and is even aggravated by it—'the power of sin is the Law' (I Cor. 15.56), though in its original intention the Law had promised life (Rom. 7.10). Sin brings us under the Divine wrath and condemnation (Rom. 1.18, 4.15) which is God's holy love reacting against evil, the 'adverse wind' of his will blowing against the sinner not only at Judgment Day but now; and, unless effectively dealt with, sin must finally prove fatal—'the wages of sin is death' (Rom. 6.23). Thus sin poses the problem of how the sinner is ever to secure the forgiveness and right standing with God which he needs if he is to regain that fellowship with God which is man's true blessedness. Here is the heart of man's predicament, nor need he think that by doing the Law he will ever cure it: 'by works of the Law will no human being be justified [counted righteous] in God's sight' (Rom. 3.20).

But in the Gospel (Paul says) the problem is solved—and solved by God, for it tells of a Divine way of getting right with God. In the Gospel 'the righteousness of God is revealed' (Rom. 1.17). When Paul as a Jew thought of 'the righteousness of God', he thought of the righteous God in action, God working out a righteous purpose, God putting things right for his people—that consummation long devoutly desired by Old Testament prophet and psalmist. Now, Paul says, in the events which make up the Gospel Story—in the Fact of Christ—God is to be openly seen doing what is needed for men's deliverance, and so making possible that new relationship with himself which men need in order to be saved.

This deliverance Paul describes in three picture-phrases: 'redemption' (*apolytrōsis*: see Rom. 3.24, Col. 1.14 and his use of the verb *eleutheroō* 'set free'); 'justification' (*dikaiōsis*: see Rom. 3.24, 4.25, 5.1 etc., Gal. 2.16 etc., Phil. 3.9); and 'reconciliation' (*katallagē*: see Rom. 5.10 f., II Cor. 5.18-20). One is a metaphor from the slave-market; the second, from the law-court; and the third, from the realm of personal relations. The first pictures an enslaved man being set free; the second, a guilty man being 'acquitted'; and the third, an estranged person being restored to favour and the family circle. All three metaphors express the way in which a gracious God delivers sinners from their sin, in Christ. When man, because of his unrighteousness, can look for nothing but condemnation, God offers him a divine righteousness in Christ. Accepting it, he gains forgiveness, a new standing with God and the power to lead a new life.

This forgiveness is grounded in the deed of the Cross. 'Christ died for our sins,' says Paul quoting the earliest *kerygma* (I Cor. 15.3). He sees the Cross in various ways: now as the supreme proof of God's love to sinners (Rom.

5.8), now as the lifting by Christ of the curse that lay upon us as breakers of the Law (Gal. 3.13), now as a victory over the demonic powers of evil (Col. 2.15). But in his two most famous passages he sees it (1) as a divinely-designed 'means of atonement' (*hilastērion*, Rom. 3.25, where the word may bear either the general meaning of 'expiation' or the more specific one of 'mercy-seat') and (2) as an act of God's appointing in which the sinless Christ, as our Representative, endured the horror of the Divine reaction against sin, that we might, in Christ, be pardoned and accepted (II Cor. 5.21).

How does sinful man make this saving work of Christ's his own? By faith—which is man's Yes, unconditional and unreserved, to the grace of God offered him in Christ. 'He who through faith is righteous, shall live', says Paul, re-interpreting the ancient words of Habakkuk (Rom. 1.17). 'By grace you have been saved through faith' (Eph. 2.8). Faith, for Paul, means taking God at his word in Christ and obeying, as once Abraham took God at his word and obeyed (Rom. 4.3 f.). Such faith is opposed to 'works', i.e. every doctrine of salvation by human effort. It is not only an act (Rom. 13.11) but an attitude—the attitude of a whole *life*: 'The life I now live in the flesh,' Paul says, 'I live by faith in the Son of God who loved me and gave himself for me' (Gal. 2.20). For the act of faith initiates a faith-union between the sinner and his Saviour (Luther likened it to a wedding ring), so that he enters into the virtue of all that Christ has done for him and lives henceforth in vital communion with his living Lord. Such faith, unless it is a sham (I Cor. 13.2), operates through love (Gal. 5.6) and issues in 'good works'. For though Paul rejected 'works' as a *condition* of salvation, no one more firmly demanded them as a *consequence* of it.

Of this faith baptism, which serves as door of entry into Christ's fellowship (I Cor. 12.3), is the *seal* (cf. Rom. 4.11).

The rite (we gather) was administered 'in the name of Christ', upon profession of faith (I Cor. 1.13, 6.11). 'You were sealed with the promised Holy Spirit,' says Paul (Eph. 1.13, II Cor. 1.22), indicating that, when at baptism a man passed into Christ's possession, he normally received the Holy Spirit as an invisible mark of authentication. But behind Christian baptism there stands for Paul (as indeed for all the apostolic writers) the One Baptism of Christ on the Cross for the sins of men; and in the actual rite, through the Spirit's action, the virtue of that Baptism is released, so that, in union with his crucified and risen Lord, the convert dies to his old life and rises into a new one (Rom. 6.3 ff., Col. 2.12. The emphasis on faith in the last passage shows that the rationale of the sacrament is to be sought in terms not of some *ex opere operato* magic but of what Wheeler Robinson has taught us to call 'prophetic symbolism'). Henceforth he is called, with the Spirit's help, to 'become what he is', a man dead to sin and alive unto God in Christ.

All this is included in what Paul means when he says, 'We were saved'.

II

But salvation is also a present and progressive experience: something happening now.

This stage can be variously described. It is being in a new realm—'the kingdom of his beloved Son' (Col. 1.13), or standing on a new platform—'this grace in which we stand' (Rom. 5.1), or enjoying a new relationship with God—that of adopted sons in God's family (Gal. 4.5). But the most positive word to describe it is 'life'—'newness of life' (Rom. 6.4), a life lived in fellowship with God through Christ, a life liberated from sin's power (the theme of Rom. 6), a life informed by 'peace with God'. This is the spiritual theory of the matter; in fact, since we are still 'in the flesh', the 'old man' is still very much alive and takes a good deal of killing. So the saved man is summoned to 'mortify' his old nature, and to become, with Divine help, the new man he potentially is.

This 'newness of life' may be further characterized as life 'in Christ' or life 'in the Spirit'.

No less than two hundred times Paul uses the phrase 'in Christ' in one or other of its forms. In some contexts it may simply be an equivalent for 'Christian' (Rom. 16.10 'Apelles the veteran Christian'; Philem. 16 'As a man and as a Christian'). But in most it means 'in communion with Christ', pregnantly describing that fellowship with a living Lord which is the very nerve of Paul's Christianity (e.g. II Cor. 12.2 'I know a man in Christ'; Phil. 4.13 'I can do all things in him who strengthens me'). Yet, if we stopped there, we should have told only half the truth, for in passage after passage the phrase carries a corporate meaning. To be 'in Christ' signifies to be 'in the community of Christ', to be a member of the new People of God of which he is the Head (e.g. Gal. 5.6 'In Christ Jesus neither circumcision nor uncircumcision is of any avail', or Rom. 8.1 'There is therefore now no condemnation for those who are in Christ Jesus'). Possibly the phrase grew out of 'baptism into Christ' (Gal. 3.27), as behind it lies the Hebrew concept of corporate personality. To be so baptized was to become a member of Christ's community: being baptized 'into Christ', men became 'in Christ'. (Note: The idea is implicit in these Synoptic sayings which stress the solidarity of the Messiah with his People, e.g. Matt. 18.20, 25.40-45.) In any case, Pauline 'mysticism' is no 'flight of the alone to the Alone'. It is a social experience. It is to have discovered the secret of true community—in Christ.

This same experience Paul describes as life 'in the Spirit', for it is through the Spirit that the living Lord comes to Christians. Theologically, Christ and the Spirit may be distinguishable (as in the apostolic benediction of II Cor. 13.14); experientially, they are one (II Cor. 3.17-18).

The Holy Spirit is the Divine *dynamic* of the new life. (Note I Thess. 1.5 and Rom. 15.13 'the power of the Holy Spirit'.) It is God's gracious power operating on and in men, though never apart from Christ. The Holy Spirit is the source not merely of what are called 'religious experiences' (like 'speaking with tongues', a gift Paul did not overvalue) but of all normal healthy religious experience. It is the Spirit which pours the love of God into our hearts (Rom. 5.5), prompts us to cry *Abba*, Father (Rom. 8.15 f.), assists our faltering prayers (Rom. 8.26), inspires the Christian graces (Gal. 5.22), enables us to fulfil the Law's demands (Rom. 8.4), and is the 'guarantee'[1] of immortal life (Rom. 8.11, II Cor. 1.22, 5.5, Eph. 1.14). The man who would know how central the Spirit is to Paul's Christianity should ponder well Gal. 5, II Cor. 3, and Rom. 8, not forgetting I Cor. 12-14 which treats of the Spirit's gifts. There the whole Christian life is Spirit-controlled. Living, suffering, praying, hoping—all is guided, prompted and secured by the strong Spirit of God.

The sphere in which the new life is lived is the Church (*Ecclēsia*).[2] With all the early Christians Paul assumes that the Church of Christ is one with the ancient People of God. (He makes this clear in his allegory of the Olive Tree in Rom. 11.17-24.) Only, the Church is the new and true *Ecclēsia*, reconstituted by Christ's death and resurrection, empowered by the Spirit, and called to a universal mission.

Basically, the Church is a pure fellowship of persons

---

[1] Greek *arrabōn*. A commercial term denoting a *down payment* which binds the purchaser to pay the total price in full.

[2] Sometimes Paul talks of '*the Ecclēsia*', sometimes of '*the ecclēsiae*', the churches. But for him the inclusive 'People-of-God' sense, deriving from the Hebrew *Qahal*, is always primary. Thus 'the church of God which is at Corinth' (I Cor. 1.2) is an outpost, or outcrop, of the one *Ecclēsia* of God.

bound to Christ, their Head, and to one another through the Holy Spirit, so that it becomes 'the Fellowship of the Spirit'. This Fellowship he describes variously: the Saints, the Temple of God, the Bride of Christ, the Household of God, etc. But his favourite name is the Body of Christ (Rom. 12.4 f., I Cor. 12.12 ff., Col. 1.18, 24, 2.19 and Ephesians *passim*). It is easy to see that the Hebrew idea of corporate personality helped Paul to think this way (Cf. Acts 9.4 'Saul, Saul, why do you persecute *me*?' suggesting that to touch Christ's followers is to touch his person). And it is a plausible guess that Paul took the name from the imagery of the Eucharist where Christians become one Body by sharing in the loaf which signifies Christ's body. 'Because there is one loaf,' Paul says (I Cor. 10.17), 'we the many [partaking of it] are one body.' It was his greatest metaphor —if indeed 'metaphor' is the right word—for it enabled Paul to portray the Church as the sphere of action of Christ's risen life. We are to think of a social organism, composed of many different members, indwelt by the living Lord, and called, by service and by suffering, to execute Christ's saving purpose in the world.

From the Church as the Body of Christ we turn to the rite which vividly illustrates it. Paul regards the Lord's Supper as the 'spiritual food and drink' of the new life (I Cor. 10.3 f.). As Baptism is the sacrament of entry into Christ's Body, so the Eucharist is the sacrament of continuing fellowship. We may observe that Paul neither undervalues nor overvalues sacraments. If a Church without them would have been inconceivable to him, he held no magical views of their efficacy. (Note in I Cor. 10.1-5 how he warns the Corinthians that the possession of sacraments confers no infallible security on those who have them.) Nevertheless he regards them not as bare symbols but as effective signs, provided always they are conjoined with faith. In the Eucharist, for example, Christians really share in the virtue of all that Christ's death has wrought for them. Indeed, the Lord's Supper is a meal with three aspects. It is a retrospect, for in the sacrament we proclaim the Lord's atoning death (I Cor. 11.26); it is a communion (*koinōnia*), for in it we share in the living Crucified with all his benefits (I Cor. 10.16 f.); and it is a prophecy, since at the meal we look away to the time when Christ will come in glory (I Cor. 11.26).

As truth for Paul was always 'truth in order to goodness', so the new life had ineluctable *moral* implications. Paul sees the good life as 'Gospel' goodness, in the sense that true Christian behaviour ought to be the spontaneous expression of the power of the Gospel in a man's life—his response, in living, of gratitude for God's grace. It is a corollary of this to say that Christian goodness was for him 'grace', and not 'law', goodness. Whereas the Law had said to Paul, 'Do these things, and you will live', the Gospel said, 'Live by God's grace and do these things'. Thus the good life appeared to him as both 'gift' and 'task'. The 'gift' was the Divine implanting of a new germ or principle of life; the 'task' was to work it out, with God's help, in a world where the insidious pulls and pressures of 'the flesh' were everywhere (cf. Phil. 2.12 f.). But what was to be the pattern of the new life? It was to be 'according to Christ' (*kata Christon*, Col. 2.18), i.e. according to all that the Fact of Christ implied and meant. So in his letters Paul elaborates various motifs for Christian living: like 'Live in a way befitting the Gospel of Christ' (Phil. 1.27), or 'Act as members of Christ's Body' (I Cor. 8, Rom. 14), or 'Fulfil the law of Christ' (Gal. 6.2) which means following Christ's example (II Cor. 8.9) and obeying his commands (I Cor. 7.10). All can be summed up in one word—*agapē*. For Paul, as for his Lord, *agapē*, the love which gives (and which may perhaps best be rendered in English 'caring'), is not only the sum-total of the Law (Rom. 13.8-10) but the master-key of morals and the supreme standard for Christian action (Phil. 2.1, Eph. 3.17 and, above all, I Cor. 13).

III

Thirdly, salvation is a future blessing: 'We shall be saved'. What does Paul teach about the Christian Hope?

Eschatology there is in plenty in his letters, for Paul, as a Jew, believed that history had a Lord, a purpose and an end. Yet he has no single, unvarying scheme of the Last Things with the time-table of events precisely charted.[1] Indeed, Paul grew in eschatological insight as he grew in grace, so that his later letters reveal a change of emphasis (especially about the *Parousia*) as compared with his earlier ones (notably I and II Thessalonians). Nevertheless, Paul held certain large and sure convictions about the Last Things which we must now set down briefly.

The first point must be that for Paul 'D-Day' has already come. Christ has died and risen, inaugurating the New Age, the Age of the Spirit. The future has, in a real sense, become present, and Christians are already enjoying the blessings of the End-time. Already 'acquitted' (justified), they do not need to wait for God's verdict on Judgment Day. Already they possess the Holy Spirit promised by the prophets for the last times. Already they are 'in the realm of God's beloved Son' (Col. 1.13).

But, secondly, since D-Day has come, the coming of V-Day, the Day of God's final victory in Christ, the *Parousia*, is sure. Amid all awareness of present blessing there always shines for Paul, like a brilliant star on the horizon, the hope of God's final consummation when 'Christ who is our life shall appear' (Col. 3.4), the Last Judgment will take place,

[1] This is the meaning of H. A. A. Kennedy's paradox: 'Paul has no eschatology' (*St Paul's Conception of the Last Things*, 20). He never wrote, systematically, *de novissimis*.

and the faithful will gain 'glory and honour and immortality' (Rom. 2.7). If earlier letters (like those to the Thessalonians) suggest that Paul expects the Day soon, his later ones (e.g. Colossians) do not stress its imminence. But, come it soon or late, it will mean the final defeat of evil and the complete triumph of God's purpose in Christ.

Thirdly, the heart of Paul's Christian Hope is to be 'with Christ' (Phil. 1.23). 'Christ, the first-born from the dead' (I Cor. 15.20) is risen and now reigns in 'the highest place that heaven affords'. What happened to him will happen to his, and 'so shall we be for ever with the Lord' (I Thess. 4.17).

The hope of being 'with Christ' hereafter depends on our being 'in Christ ' now. What then will be the fate of those who reject him? In II Thessalonians[1] he predicts eternal destruction' for the disobedient. Later, in Romans, as also in the Prison Epistles, he moves forward to some kind of 'larger Hope'. 'God,' he says, 'has shut up all men unto disobedience, that he may have mercy upon all' (Rom. 10.32). Does this mean that Paul was a 'universalist' in the dogmatic sense of the word? We may reasonably doubt it. Here Paul is thinking in terms of races, not of individuals, and elsewhere (e.g. II Cor. 2.15 f.) he clearly envisages the possibility of men 'perishing'.

Fourthly, the mode of the Christian's heavenly life will be a 'spiritual body'. A 'resurrection of relics' Paul repudiates (I Cor. 15.50). For him, the body (*sōma*) means the principle of self-identity persisting through all changes of substance, so that 'personality' is perhaps our nearest modern equivalent. Now, the body has a material means of embodiment; hereafter—for immortality is the gift of God, not a natural possession of man—God will give it a spiritual

---

[1] II Thess. 1.9. Eternal destruction is the opposite of 'eternal life' and means separation from God for ever. See W. Neil, *Thessalonians*, 149.

means of expression befitting the supernal world. Our 'lowly bodies' will be changed to resemble Christ's 'glorious body' (Phil. 3.21), that body invested with the splendour of another world which Paul had himself seen on the Damascus Road.

When does this change come? In the Thessalonian correspondence, as in I Cor. 15, Paul looks for it at the Day of Christ. In II Cor. 5.1-10,[1] his thought apparently changing because in the interval he had been brought face to face with death, he expects it when he dies, and in Phil. 1.23 he speaks of 'departing and being with Christ' (Judaism thought of the Age to Come both as the End of history and as an eternally existent order). But let the change come when it will, the final redemption of the body is certain (Rom. 8.23).

In his teaching about the Last Things Paul is well aware that 'we know only in part', that our earthly vision of these realities is like peering through an unclear mirror (I Cor. 13.9-12). But of one thing he is invincibly sure, that nothing in the world or out of it will be able to separate us from the love of God in Christ (Rom. 8.38 f.). Beyond this he does not go. It is enough to know that 'this corruptible must put on incorruption, and this mortal, immortality' (I Cor. 15.53).

'And with God be the rest.'

IV

What place did Paul give Christ in the ways of God with men? There is truth in Deissmann's dictum that Paul is not so much the great *Christologos* as the great *Christophorus*

---

[1] So Charles, Windisch, Howard, etc. Others deny that Paul's view changed. What is not doubtful in this obscure passage is Paul's conviction that death, if it comes, will mean seeing his Lord and being at home with him.

—his mission was not so much to expound the mysteries of Christ's person as to persuade men to accept his benefits. But you cannot proclaim salvation, as Paul did, without also making assertions and claims for the Saviour.

Let us start, then, by saying that Paul's Gospel is Christocentric. All centres in him. This does not mean, however, that for Paul Christ has usurped the place of God. Rather, it is God who confronts men in Christ, the same God who once acted in creation: 'It is the God who said, Let light shine out of darkness, who has shone in our hearts to give the light of the knowledge of the glory of God in the face of Christ' (II Cor. 4.6). In Paul's view, this God is savingly known to men only in Christ; for in him God draws near to sinners and stretches out his rescuing hand. And this Christ, as every page of Paul's writing attests, is no mere figure in past history but a living and delivering Presence who dwells in the believer's heart through the power of the Holy Spirit.

Did then Paul know little and care less about the Jesus whom we know from the Gospels? This would be a capital mistake to make. The fact that he does not say more is easily explicable on three main grounds: Paul's readers already knew the main facts about Jesus: the Epistles are Epistles, not Gospels: and Paul's gaze is naturally enough fixed on the living and exalted Lord. Yet in fact, quite incidentally, we can glean enough from his letters to write (as Renan said) a brief life of Christ. We learn, first, that Jesus was a man (Gal. 4.4), born of David's line (Rom. 1.3), and having brothers (I Cor. 9.5); that his ministry was to the Jews (Rom. 15.8) and his lot that of a poor man (II Cor. 8.9); that, before the Jews killed him (I Thess. 2.15), he instituted the Lord's Supper (I Cor. 11.23 ff.); and that, after crucifixion and burial, he was raised on the third day and exalted to heaven (I Cor. 15.3 ff., Phil. 2.9). The character of the man is also known. He was gentle and meek (II Cor. 10.1), obedient to his Father's will (Phil. 2.8), unacquainted with sin (II Cor. 5.21) and the embodiment of love (I Cor. 13.4 ff.).[1] As for his teaching Paul can quote his sayings when the occasion demands it, and the ethical parts of his letters (e.g. Rom. 12.14 where there are eight distinct echoes of Christ's words) are permeated with the teaching of his Lord.

In any account of his Christology the first important point to seize is that, for Paul, as for all the New Testament writers, Jesus was at once human and divine. He was truly human in that he 'was born of a woman, born under the law' (Gal. 4.4 Cf. I Cor. 15.21) and came 'in the likeness of sinful flesh' (Rom. 8.3), that is, his humanity was real but sinless. No less certainly, however, Paul sets Jesus on that side of reality we call divine, naming him—as witness the salutations of the epistles—in the same breath with God the Father and applying to him words which in the Old Testament had been applied to God. In short, for Paul, Jesus is the God-man in whom 'dwells the plenitude of deity, corporeally' (Col. 2.9).[2]

When we review the titles Paul applies to Jesus, we note that he never calls him 'the Son of man' (though it may underlie a passage like I Cor. 15.27) and very rarely the Messiah (Rom. 9.5 is the only certain example): not because Paul did not believe Jesus to be the Messiah but because such language would have conveyed nothing to Gentile ears. We might have expected to find the title 'Saviour' oftener than twice (Phil. 3.20, Eph. 5.23); but Paul clearly preferred the title 'Lord' (*Kyrios*) which occurs everywhere in his letters and which not only spoke mean-

---

[1] Can we doubt who it was sat in the studio of Paul's imagination for this portrait? As in George Herbert's poem, 'Love bade me welcome', we might for 'love' write 'Christ'.

[2] The only passage in which Paul seems to call Christ 'God' is Rom. 9.5: 'Christ . . . who is over all, God blessed for ever.' But many scholars agree with the R.S.V. in translating here: 'Christ. God who is over all be blessed for ever.'

ing-fully to Gentile ears, accustomed to 'lords many', but conferred on Jesus a spiritual rank which demanded worship. Alongside the title 'Lord' we may set the other one, 'Son of God', which he uses seventeen times. In some cases it may be no more than a synonym for Messiah; but where Paul speaks of 'his Son' or God's 'own Son' (Gal. 4.4, Rom. 8.32, Col. 1.13) he obviously is thinking of Jesus as God's Son in a unique and unshared sense, the sense indeed which was in Jesus' own mind when once he sought to disclose the secret of his person to his disciples (Matt. 11.27, Q.).

Equally significant are the categories in which Paul tried to set forth the theological significance of Jesus for his readers: the Second Adam, the new *Torah*, the Divine Wisdom. As Paul thought of Christianity as the new creation, so he spoke of Christ (Rom. 5 and I Cor. 15) as the Second (or last) Adam, meaning thus to set Christ forth as the Head of the new redeemed Humanity as Adam had been of the old unredeemed. Though Paul never says in so many words, 'Christ is the new *Torah*', it is impossible to deny that he so thought of Jesus. 'Conformity to Christ, his teaching and his life,' W. D. Davies has written, 'has taken the place for Paul of conformity to the Jewish *Torah*. Jesus himself—in word and deed or fact—is a New *Torah*'.[1] The proof lies in passages like II Cor. 3.7 ff. and Rom. 10.6 ff. (where Paul takes words from Deut. 30.12 ff., originally referring to the Law, and applies them to Christ). What did the *Torah* mean for the Jew? It meant 'all that God has made known of his nature, character and purpose and of what he would have man be and do'.[2] So Paul regarded Christ as the complete revelation, in flesh and blood, of God's nature and will for man.

Finally, Paul spoke of Jesus as the Divine Wisdom (I

[1] *Paul and Rabbinic Judaism*, 148.
[2] G. F. Moore, *Judaism*, I, 263.

Cor. 1.24, 30, Col. 1.15). The ultimate source of this doctrine is Prov. 8 where the figure of Wisdom is conceived as pre-existent and as God's agent in creation. In using this figure of Divine Wisdom to express what the Fact of Christ meant for him, Paul sought to show not only his belief in Christ's pre-existence (which he implies elsewhere) but chiefly his conviction that the created universe bears the marks of the Saviour, that to live 'after Christ' is the natural life, and that ultimately Nature and Grace are two sides of one Divine medal.

Such titles and categories—and we have by no means exhausted them—show how the apostle ransacked language and thought to set forth the absolute significance of Christ. In him he had found 'unsearchable riches'. Through him he had gained access to the unseen Father. In his face he had seen shining the glory of the ineffable God. What wonder then if he believed that Christ's story did not begin at Bethlehem, that the Fact of Christ was embedded in the constitution of creation itself, and that all time and history were moving on to Christ?

'MY GOSPEL'

Reading Paul's letters we light, from time to time, on phrases like 'my Gospel' or 'the Gospel that I preach', suggesting something unshared with any other apostle, something indefeasibly his own. Yet it has been our vigorous contention that, basically, Paul's Gospel was the common apostolic Gospel. What was there, then (if anything) distinctive about Christianity according to St Paul?

Let us begin our answer with the obvious point that Paul, being the kind of man he was, could not take over anything without setting his own stamp upon it. In our sketch of Primitive Christianity we noticed how this or that passage in Paul's letters could be labelled 'pre-Pauline' or 'traditional', and at the start of this chapter we listed no less than seven items which might fairly be reckoned among Paul's debts to his Christian predecessors: *credenda* he had 'received' from those 'in Christ' before him. But Paul, being Paul, was never content merely to receive anything and leave it as he got it, like the servant with his talent in the parable. Three examples will be enough.

Consider, first, the apostolic Gospel. We have Paul's own word for it (in I Cor. 15.11) that the *kerygma* which he preached did not differ from that of the Jerusalem apostles. But since (as a great master of the art has defined it) preaching is 'truth through personality', and since Paul's was no ordinary personality, the common apostolic Gospel inevitably came from Paul's lips enriched and deepened by his own insights and experiences. No doubt every apostolic preacher presented the Gospel as a message of salvation from sin; but who among them diagnosed man's spiritual malaise with the acuteness and penetration exhibited in the first and seventh chapters of Romans? Every apostolic preacher believed that 'Christ died for our sins according to the scriptures'; but we should need a good deal of persuading that they all revealed the profound understanding of the Cross that we find, say, in Rom. 5 and II Cor. 5.14-21. Every apostolic preacher proclaimed the Resurrection; but not every one could high-light his witness to the risen Lord with the moving personal testimony of the Damascus Road.

Or consider the person of the Saviour. Paul's Christian predecessors worshipped Jesus as Messiah, Lord and Son of God. But who before Paul dared to apply to Christ the breath-taking language of Col. 1.15 ff. with its claim that the Fact of Christ is embedded in the created universe, that it is all there with Christ in view, and in some deep mysterious way has the promise of Christ in it? If we may not say that Paul preached a bigger Christ than his predecessors, we may surely claim that he was the first to grasp the true magnitude of his person, compelled as he was by the Colossian heretics and others to relate the Saviour to the religious needs not of Judaism only but of the great Gentile world.

Or take the universality of the Gospel. It may well be that Paul was not the first to glimpse the world-mission of the Church or realize that the new Israel was to be 'a light to lighten the Gentiles'. Stephen probably saw this too when he argued that God's call to Israel had always been 'Go out' and named Jesus 'the Son of man' whose dominion was to embrace all peoples, nations and tongues (Dan. 7.13 f.). But who before Paul saw with such utter clarity the universal, even cosmic, scope of the salvation wrought in Christ (as we see it, for example, in the Epistle to the Ephesians) or summoned the Church so magnificently to what we may call its ecumenical mission?

These things apart, what was Paul's most distinctive contribution to the understanding of the Gospel?

Our answer would be that it fell to Paul, the ex-Pharisee, to interpret the Fact of Christ in terms of *righteousness*. In other words, his most distinctive doctrine was 'justification by faith' There is good reason to believe (as we shall see in our chapter on Petrine Christianity) that Paul was not quite the first to teach this doctrine; but we may truly say of Paul that

> *in his hand the thing became a trumpet*
> *Whence he blew soul-animating strains.*[1]

The doctrine occurs mainly in Romans, Galatians, and Philippians, i.e. generally in polemic with Judaisers, so that we may call it a 'doctrine of conflict'. Let us state it shortly. For Paul, as for the devout Pharisee, the vital question was: How shall a sinful man get right with the holy God? With the Pharisee Paul agreed in this: No righteousness (*dikaio-*

[1] Wordsworth.

synē), no salvation. With the Pharisee he agreed also in taking righteousness to mean not primarily ethical perfection but acceptance with God. 'Righteousness is the Yea spoken by God on a man's life'. It was on the question of *how* that righteousness was to be obtained that Paul finally parted company with the Pharisee. While still himself a Pharisee, Paul had believed that the secret lay in the punctilious observance of the Law of Moses. Only let a man fully keep its requirements, and righteousness would be his. 'Do these things,' ran the theory, 'and you will live.' But, by bitter experience, Paul found that this road led nowhere. For various reasons, the chief of which was 'the power of sin in the flesh', this road to righteousness proved a *cul-de-sac*. Instead of producing righteousness, the Law exposed him as a sinner, and drove him to despair (Rom. 7).

Then he met Christ, and from that decisive encounter came the answer to his question. God (he found) had provided a totally different way of deliverance. 'Not by works of Law but by faith in Christ,' was the secret. Righteousness—God's, not his own, a gift of God's grace in Christ and not a product of man's strenuous moral endeavour—became his on the sole condition of faith in the Christ who, by God's appointing, had died for his sins. Now he found what he had sought vainly in the Law, a new and right relationship with God, which brought pardon, peace and joy. Deliverance from sin and its consequences was God's work, not man's, a gift and not an achievement.

This, then, was Paul's sovereign truth, and it is important to notice that here he is at one with his Lord. Both Jesus and Paul agree that no man is so far from God as the self-righteous person. If Jesus says, 'It is the beggars before God who are blessed' (Matt. 5.3), Paul says, 'God justifies the ungodly' (Rom. 4.5). And not only has Jesus given us in the great parable of the Gracious Father (Luke 15.11-32) an imperishable account of what Paul means by 'God justifying the ungodly', but in that other parable of the Pharisee and the Publican (Luke 18.10-14) he teaches the same truth and describes God's acceptance of the sinner with Paul's very word, 'justified' (*dikaiousthai*).

Two things, then, in Paul's doctrine are of enduring importance.

First, he insisted that true religion is a matter of a right relationship with God. It is not primarily a matter of ethics and moral striving. Were it so, wisdom would work out the rules of conduct (as the rabbis did) and order you to observe them in every detail, as you would be saved. But Paul said (and the experience of countless people since his day confirms it) that such a method would never bring a man where he wanted to be.

Second, Paul made this right relationship depend wholly on faith in God's historic act in Christ. A man's salvation is solely due to God's gracious action in Christ—that, and his faith in it. So Paul found the answer to the question that haunted him so long—found it for himself and found it for others. By so doing, he safeguarded the Gospel from degenerating into legalism, or mere mysticism, or formal sacramentalism. And this is why Paul, being dead these nineteen hundred years, still speaks to us to-day, and will speak as long as Christianity claims the interest of men.

6

ST PETER

PETER and Paul are the great names among the apostles. Paul's theology we know. But can we know anything of Peter's? Did the two apostles differ? Or did they fundamentally agree?

It is too simple to reply, 'Have we not, for comparison, two Epistles of Peter in the New Testament?' For only extreme conservatives ascribe II Peter to St Peter, and many excellent scholars deny even I Peter to him. A better approach to an answer is by way of two statements in St Paul's letters. In I Cor. 15.1-11, after quoting the Gospel 'tradition' he had 'received', Paul declares: 'Whether then it was I or they, in these terms we preach, and in these terms you believed'. This is a clear claim that on the basic Gospel facts agreement existed between himself and the original Jerusalem apostles ('they'), among whom Peter ranked as a 'pillar'. But this is not all. When the two apostles had their famous 'words' about table-fellowship at Antioch (some time in the late 'forties'), Paul declared emphatically that Peter's understanding of salvation did not differ from his own. 'We,' he said to Peter, 'we know that a man is not justified by works of the law but through faith in Jesus Christ' (Gal. 2.16). What does this mean? That 'justification by faith' is not a doctrine of Paul's discovering (as many suppose), even if he gave it a central place? Yes, but also that Peter's doctrine was basically the same as Paul's.

If the two apostles agreed (1) on the main Gospel facts, and (2) on the basic idea of salvation, should we not expect that, if any letter of Peter has survived in the New Testament, it would be, theologically, not unlike one of St Paul's? And should we not expect the resemblance to be still closer if we had reason to suppose that an old colleague of Paul's had helped Peter to write it?

The New Testament preserves just such a letter claiming to be Peter's (a claim never disputed in the early Church) and to have been written with the help of Silvanus (5.12. Silas is short for Silvanus). It contains some things that strongly remind us of St Paul (e.g. phrases like 'the God of all grace', the formula 'in Christ' etc.), as its basic understanding of the Fact of Christ is the same. But it has other traits which justify the verdict that the writer is 'no Pauline'. This is precisely what we should expect. The fact is that one of the objections often made to Petrine authorship of the letter, its 'Paulinism', collapses when we realize that a great deal of what we once called 'Paulinism' is common apostolic Christianity. Another objection—that a Galilean fisherman could not have written the good Greek of the Epistle—is no more cogent if we remember that Silvanus, whose command of Greek must have matched Paul's, was Peter's amanuensis. Only if it could be proved (and nobody has as yet proved it) that not till the beginning of the second century did men 'suffer as Christians' (4.16), should we have to surrender Peter's connexion with the letter. We conclude that I Peter is the work of Peter-cum-Silvanus, that it came from Rome (the 'Babylon' of 5.13) on the eve of the Neronian persecution, and that it was an encyclical letter[1] designed to nerve the mainly Gentile

---

[1] *Note.* The theory of Perdelwitz, Streeter, Beare and F. L. Cross that I Pet. is pseudonymous and that in it we are to find a baptismal sermon (1.3-4.11) combined with another letter to a persecuted community (4.12-5.11) is unconvincing. (1) It arbitrarily dismisses the epistolary salutation at the beginning and the *personalia* at the end as late fictions; (2) it makes a complete break between 1.3-4.11 and 4.12-5.11, though the sufferings of 1.6 are clearly those of 4.12; and (3) it forces baptismal meanings on quite general passages.

Christians of Asia Minor to endure bravely whatever suffering might befall them.

CHRISTIANITY ACCORDING TO ST PETER

With all this the theology of the letter accords, as we may see if we consider how it presents the Fact of Christ.

The earliest Christians believed that, if the Gospel was 'new' News, it was also 'old' News in the sense that it had been prefigured in the ancient prophecies. This is the point of I Peter 1.10-12 and 24-25. The Fact of Christ fulfils the Divinely-inspired insights of the prophets, and the Gospel is that very 'living and lasting Word of God' which came to Isaiah.

Jesus the Messiah who was 'destined before the foundation of the world', has been 'manifested at the end of times' (1.20). But the Messiah took the form of the Servant of the Lord who 'bore our sins in his own body on the tree' (2.22-24. In Acts Peter calls Jesus 'God's servant' and the Cross a 'tree'). Like a paschal lamb without blemish and spot, he 'ransomed' us by his sacrifice (1.18 f.), dying for our sins 'the just for the unjust' that he might procure us access to God (3.18). He descended into Hades (3.19 f. Cf. Acts 2.27, 31).

But God raised him from the dead and 'gave him glory' (1.3, 21. Cf. Peter in Acts 3.13 'The God of our fathers glorified his servant Jesus'), so that he is now 'the Lord' (2.3, 3.15. Cf. Peter in Acts 2.36 'God has made him both Lord and Christ'). The Holy Spirit has been sent from heaven upon the apostles (1.12). And now the new Israel, inheriting the titles and status of old Israel (2.9-10), declares God's mighty acts to men, and awaits the time when Christ shall be unveiled in glory (1.7, 13, 4.13, 5.1, 4).

Here are the very accents of the apostolic preaching.[1] True, we are now in the early 'sixties' of the first century, and the Church has made its astonishing leap into the great Gentile world, so that it now numbers more Gentiles than Jews in its membership; but the Gospel remains the same indefeasibly Jewish thing it was from the start—as witness the Old Testament types and analogues used to interpret Christ's person and work. Mark too the eschatological tension—the sense of living 'between the times': on the one hand, the conviction that with the coming of the Messiah and his Church the *eschaton* has entered history: on the other, the persuasion that, because this is so, the final consummation cannot be long delayed.

From his understanding of the Fact of Christ flows Peter's view of Christian salvation.

He describes the beginning of the Christian life as a new birth given by God to men through his Word (1.23). Then God 'called them out of darkness into his marvellous light' (2.9), and they returned from aimless wandering to the care of the Good Shepherd (2.25). Of this event the saving sign is Baptism, whose importance lies not in physical cleansing but in the convert's 'pledge to God from a clear conscience'[2] (3.21). This sounds like the public profession at baptism of that faith which is man's response to God's gracious dealing with him in the Gospel.

Faith, for Peter, is faith in God through Christ as mediator (note 1.21 'who through him believe in God'); and what Peter means by faith we may best learn from 1.8. It is love of, and trust in, the unseen Saviour, bringing with it great joy. If that faith is genuine, suffering should only serve to refine it, and its end will be complete salvation (1.7, 9).

---

[1] i.e. *kerygma*. As for *didachē*, note how 'Words of the Lord' are quoted or echoed in ethical contexts: 1.17, 2.12, 19 f., 3.9, 14, 5.6, 7.
[2] See E. G. Selwyn, *The First Epistle of Peter*, 205.

The new birth is birth into the new life of the Church. Though he never uses the word *ecclēsia*, nothing could be clearer than Peter's conviction that the Church is the new Israel, the true People of God (2.10). The images he uses to describe it are simple, vivid, pictorial, recalling Christ's own words about it. It is the Flock of God in which Christ is the chief Shepherd (2.25, 5.2-4); it is the new Spirit-filled Sanctuary where the living Christ occupies the head of the corner and believers are built in as living stones (2.4 ff.); it is God's Household or Family (4.17). The role of the Church is both priestly and prophetic: priestly, because it is called to 'offer spiritual sacrifices acceptable to God through Jesus Christ'; prophetic, because summoned to 'declare the excellence of him who called them out of darkness into his marvellous light' (2, 5, 9).

The present life of Christians is a life 'in grace', since theirs is 'the God of all grace' (5.10, 12). 'Sanctified by the Spirit' which 'rests upon' them (1.2, 4.14), they are meant to 'grow up to salvation', coming continually to the Lord and tasting his kindness (2.2 ff.). Not that they can expect immunity from suffering: it is the constant theme of the letter that, as Christ has suffered for them, they must be ready to share his sufferings (2.18-21, 4.13). But such sufferings, bravely borne, will not only disarm pagan critics but win God's favour (2.20, 3.16). Christianity means an *anastrophē*—a way of life. Jesus 'died to make us good' (cf. 2.24), and we are called as 'obedient children' to a life of holiness (1.14 f.), purity (2.11), humility (5.6) and love (1.22, 2.17, 4.8). The Christian will 'maintain good conduct' among his pagan neighbours, preserve a high and honourable family life, and use his gifts as 'a good steward of God's varied grace' (4.10).

The end of grace is 'glory', a favourite word of Peter's for future blessedness. This is the 'living hope' created by Christ's Resurrection (1.3), which sustains Christians on their pilgrim way (1.1, 17, 2.11) and enables them to rejoice in suffering. History is moving to its appointed *dénouement* when Christ will be unveiled in glory (1.7, 13, 4.13, 5.1, 4) and the Father will judge all men (1.17, 4.5).

In two passages Peter hints that the scope of redemption is not limited to this life. 'The Gospel was preached even to the dead' we read (4.6), and again, 'Christ went [between his death and resurrection] and preached to the spirits in prison' (3.18 f.), by whom he apparently means the wicked contemporaries of Noah. Whatever we make of these dark passages, they embody a conviction, which we may well share, that, wherever men are, Christ has power to save.

It is not, however, on the fate of the lost but on the blessedness of the redeemed that Peter dwells. The reward of perseverant faith is 'an unwithering crown of glory' (5.4) in that 'inheritance, imperishable, undefiled and unfading, kept in heaven for them' (1.4).

Luther was right. I Peter, though short, is 'a powerful, rich epistle'. The circumstances to which Peter addressed himself may differ *toto caelo* from those in which we find ourselves. But in a secularized world like ours where men and women often live under the tyranny of laws which make it 'very hard to be a Christian', his letter has not lost its relevance. We too are called not only to witness for Christ by the silent testimony of our lives, but to 'give a reason for the hope that is in us', as we are summoned (in Maeterlinck's words) to 'live as always on the threshold of great joy'.

7

THE WRITER TO THE HEBREWS

THIS interpreter we shall call *Auctor* (the Writer) because, as Origen observed long ago, his real name is known only to God. If he was not Apollos, as Luther guessed, he was somebody very like the Jewish Christian from Alexandria described in Acts 18.24 f. In view of his Platonized Judaism and love of allegory, it is not unlikely that he wrote from Alexandria. His readers, on the likelier interpretation of 13.24,[1] lived in Rome.

We take them to be Jewish Christians in the capital who, threatened with persecution, would fain have shrunk back under cover of the Jewish religion, a religion permitted by Rome as Christianity was not.[2] Living too much in the Jewish part of their faith, they remained backwardly blind to the true horizons of their Christian calling. By contrast, *Auctor* was a man of the same wide, forward-looking vision as Stephen (Acts 7). Like him, he had glimpsed the universal significance of the Fact of Christ and knew that the Church had a world mission.

On this view many things in the letter become luminous: *Auctor's* call to the new Exodus (3.7-19) and the pilgrim life of faith (11); his theological proof that the new means of grace brought by Christ offer the reality which the old means of grace could only faintly foreshadow; his warnings against 'shrinking back' (10.38 f.), and his challenge to them to 'go forth to Jesus outside the camp, bearing his reproach' (13.13).

[1] 'Those who come from Italy send you greetings' (R.S.V.).
[2] William Manson, *The Epistle to the Hebrews* (1951).

The letter must have been written before the Fall of Jerusalem in A.D. 70. The Temple seems still to be standing (8.4, 9.6, 10.1): had it fallen when *Auctor* wrote, he must have pointed to the fact as proof conclusive that God had no further use for this focus of the ancient sanctities. Two persecutions are mentioned, one past, and one impending. The first (10.32 f.) we take to be the trouble which arose in the Roman synagogues when the Gospel found an entrance there, and the Emperor cleared the Jews out of the capital (A.D. 49).[1] The second (12.3 ff.) represents the first moves against the Christians which culminated in the red martyrdom of 64. All suggests a date about 63.

CHRISTIANITY ACCORDING TO 'THE AUTHOR'

I

So difficult is Hebrews for the modern reader that we shall start with an outline of the letter itself. It consists of an Exordium (1.1-4), an Argument (1.5-10.18), an Application (10.19-12.29) and a Conclusion (13).

The Exordium states the theme: God has made a final revelation of himself in his Son.

Then begins the Argument, diversified by admonitions (2.1-4; 3.7-4.13; 5.11-6.20). Jesus Christ is God's final revelation because in his person he is Son and in his work he is Priest. First, *Auctor* sets forth Jesus as the Son. As such, he excels the angels, mediators of the old revelation, and is superior to Moses as a son is to a servant. Then (4.14) he begins to describe the Son's work as a Priest. Jesus is a divinely appointed High Priest of that Melchizedek 'order' which antiquates the Levitical priesthood. He

[1] 'He expelled the Jews from Rome when they made a constant rioting at the instigation of Chrestus.' (Suetonius.)

is also one who has known our human trials. Divine appointment and human sympathy make him indeed the perfect High Priest (7). He ministers in the perfect sanctuary (heaven: 8). And he offers the perfect sacrifice (9).[1] This offering, being that of his own flawless obedience to God's will, avails to take away men's sins as the blood of beasts could never do, and the boon which priestly work brings to men is that of 'access' to God's presence.

After the Argument comes the Application (10.19). Since the great High Priest has opened up this new 'access' to the Divine presence, they must avail themselves of it, or take the fearful consequences of their refusal. Let them remember that they stand in the great succession of the heroes of faith, whose quest for the City of God has now been fulfilled in Jesus. Any suffering they may endure is part of God's disciplining of them as sons, and the glories of the Old Covenant are not worthy to be compared with those of the New.

Then comes the Conclusion, with counsels, warnings and a noble benediction.

From this high discourse we have to discover the main features of *Auctor's* Christianity, and straightway we may say three things about it.

First, his Christianity keeps living touch with the earliest evangel. With a little study it is not hard to disentangle the outline of the *kerygma*:

The prophecies have been fulfilled in God's revelation in his Son (1.1).
He is Jesus the Messiah of David's line (7.14) and the Heir (1.2).

---

[1] Perfect, because it is of himself (not an external sacrifice), because it is without blemish (Christ was sinless), and because it was offered 'through eternal spirit' (Christ was immortal, so that his sacrifice has eternal value. 9.11-14).

He came into the world to do God's will (10.7) and declare the message of salvation (2.3).

In order to 'bear the sins of many' he, 'by the grace of God', 'endured the Cross' (9.28, 2.9, 12.2).

God raised him from the dead (13.20).

He is now at God's right hand (1.3, 13, etc.).

A little while, and he will appear a second time (9.28, 10.25, 37).

Hence the need for repentance, faith and baptism (6.1 f.).

Basic, then, to *Auctor's* theology is the primitive evangel with Jewish eschatology at its heart; but the observant reader soon detects another element. Sometimes, as in 8.1-5, *Auctor* works with 'a two-storey view of reality' reminiscent of Plato and his parable of the cave-dwellers and the shadows in the seventh book of the *Republic*. The ground-floor is the world of the shadowy and transitory; the upper storey is the world of the real and eternal. Thus the true sanctuary which is set up not by man but by the Lord is in heaven, and of this heavenly reality the earthly tent is but a copy and shadow (8.2, 5, 9.23). The Old Covenant (*Auctor* argues) gave us only the shadow of these supernal realities; under the New Covenant the realities themselves have invaded this world of time and sense, since Christ is 'the High Priest of the good things that have come' (9.11).[1] Thus Plato is 'impressed' to serve Christ.

Our third point concerns *Auctor's* mode of thinking. For him, the heart of true religion consists in 'access' to God, an access functioning through worship (4.16, 7.25, 10.22, 12.22). But sin hinders this access, marring that communion with God which is man's *summum bonum*. If man is ever to attain it, he must somehow 'get through' to God. But how? The ritual of the Jewish law—the whole system of

[1] Reading *genomenōn* (with P 46 B D, etc.), not *mellontōn*. So R.S.V.

priest and sanctuary and sacrifice—undertook to bring him there. Alas, it could not. It might purify the flesh, but it could not cleanse the conscience. Christianity is the final religion because, through Christ's sacrifice, it secures the access which Judaism could only shadow forth. With the Fact of Christ we pass 'out of the world of shadows into the realm of reality'.

II

Like all the apostolic writers, *Auctor* holds a three-tensed doctrine of salvation. Salvation began when we heard 'the good news' and were 'enlightened' (4.2, 6.4). Then we 'tasted the heavenly gift, became partakers of the Holy Spirit, experienced how good the Gospel is, and shared in the powers of the age to come' (6.4 f.).

Salvation in its present aspect *Auctor* sees as a treading of the pilgrim way pioneered by Christ. On this road we have the help of the Holy Spirit (2.4, 6.4), we enjoy our new Christ-won access to God's presence, and we are watched by an unseen host (12.1). Not alone but in the company of God's People (4.9, 8.10) we make the journey, and we look on and away to Jesus who has finished the course (12.2).

No New Testament writer has more grandly pictured the journey's end, the final 'Rest' of God's People. Christ will come in glory to establish the eternal kingdom. For our true homeland is above, the heavenly Jerusalem where amid the angels and the redeemed sit our Father and Judge and that Son whose death has procured us *entrée* into his Presence (12.22 f.).

Of this 'eternal salvation' the 'mediator' is Jesus. No apostolic writer has a higher conception of Christ's divinity or a truer appreciation of the real-ness of his humanity. Set the opening verses of Hebrews against 5.7, and the polarities of his Christological thinking become clear: on the one hand, the Man who 'offered up prayers and supplications with loud cries and tears to him who was able to save him from death'; on the other, the Son, the universal Heir, who radiates God's glory because he 'bears the very stamp of his nature, upholding the universe by the word of his power'. Clearly our Author cherishes two firm convictions, that Christ was a man who knew our human lot and was tempted as we are, and that God himself came down to us through him, once for all and for ever.

How does this theology compare with Paul's? *Auctor* has his doctrine of 'access', but he lacks Paul's 'in Christ' mysticism. His concept of faith is different, as his stress on the humanity and suffering of Christ is characteristically his own. But we must not exaggerate the differences when we recall that so acute a Biblical scholar as Origen judged *Auctor's* thoughts Pauline, when we note that what he means by 'sanctify' is precisely what Paul means by 'justify', and when we reflect that 'Christ the High Priest over the House of God' is really only another way of saying 'Christ the Head of the Body'.

The word 'hieratical' perhaps best sums up the distinctive thing in his theology. Hebrews is the only book in the New Testament which contains a complete theory of the Atonement couched in priestly and sacrificial terms. As we have seen, the heart of what he says is that Christ is the ideal High Priest who has offered the ideal sacrifice in the ideal sanctuary. What was it in Christ's sacrifice that gave it its atoning power? *Auctor's* answer would seem to be that it was the perfect obedience of the Son to his Father's will when faced with the problem of human sin. It was his intelligent and loving response to that will so that, in his representative death for men, he took upon himself the burden and doom of our sin and bore it away. Christ's is therefore the 'one true, pure, immortal sacrifice' which has cleansed

God's People from their sin and made them fit for the Divine Presence; and in the power of that sacrifice he has passed into the heavenly sanctuary where he ever lives to intercede for them.

III

Much in this letter has only an antiquarian interest for us to-day: the minutiae of the Levitical cultus, the allegorizing exegesis, the play made with an obscure Old Testament character like Melchizedek, etc. Nevertheless, Hebrews sounds certain notes which contain a permanent appeal and challenge.

We begin with the *priestly* note. Even those who would scorn to be called 'High Churchmen' must feel the fascination of *Auctor's* world in which everything is dominated by the great High Priest, seated at the right hand of the Majesty on high, clothed in our nature, compassionate to our weaknesses, pleading our cause. And, all sacerdotal arguments apart, we need our Author's doctrine of Christ's heavenly intercession as the necessary complement to faith in his atoning death.

Only the rabidly sectarian will think discordant the *ecumenical* note which William Manson has rediscovered in the letter. If we will, *Auctor* may teach us the unwisdom of clinging fearfully to ancient forms of worship when the clarion call to-day is for men to carry Christ's empire to the furthest confines of the world.

Timely, too, is the *pilgrim* note, heard supremely in the bede-roll of chapter 11 where the heroes are no mere wandering adventurers but men in search of the City of God.

The badge they share is faith, which is a 'venturing upon vision'. True, its basic meaning is assurance of the reality of the unseen verities (11.1); but it is assurance adventuring and enduring, as Abraham, Moses and the rest down to the

Maccabean martyrs adventured and endured. In Jesus the end of their quest is to be seen. He is faith's mightiest Captain who has pioneered a new and living way, whereby we too may travel

> *On to the end of the road*
> *On to the City of God.*[1]

[1] M. Arnold.

8

ST JOHN

MANY would call St John the greatest of the interpreters. Standing farthest from the event, he saw it in its most abiding significance, so that Christ appears no longer merely as a figure in past history but as the great Contemporary. 'The Jesus of history,' it is as if John were saying to us, 'is the Christ of experience. What he is now to my faith, that he was in the days of his flesh.' And all down the centuries he has so communicated something of his secret to his readers that his Gospel still speaks to the condition of sage and simple, serving at once as 'the text-book of the parish priest' and a divine philosophy for a Wordsworth or a Westcott.

ST JOHN, HIS BOOKS AND HIS BACKGROUND

But who was John, and where did he write, and when? We need not dwell long on the second and third questions. It is generally agreed that the Gospel and three Epistles of John originated in Ephesus about the last decade of the first century. It is further agreed that their writer was not John the Seer of the Apocalypse. Despite some distinguished demurrers (including C. H. Dodd), it is commonly held that the four documents are the work of one man who, in II and III John, calls himself 'the Elder'. If nowadays few are found defending the full apostolic authorship of the Fourth Gospel, most would agree that 'the Beloved Disciple' and the Witness (19.35) may well be John the Apostle whose testimony would therefore underlie the Gospel. Who then was 'the Elder'? He may have been John the Elder to whose existence Papias testifies. The Fourth Gospel, at any rate, suggests that its writer was a disciple of the Apostle and had himself firm links with Palestine. The accuracy of his Palestinian topography, his knowledge of Jewish customs and his Semitized Greek point strongly to an Aramaic-speaking Jew who had lived in Palestine before he settled in Ephesus. Probably the traditions about Jesus which he used in his Gospel had been carried by him to Asia Minor before the Fall of Jerusalem in A.D. 70.[1]

With all this the Gospel itself agrees. To be sure, St John shows himself far more aware of Greek thought than St Paul does; and when we encounter the word *logos* in the first verse of his Gospel, we may suppose that we are about to see the Gospel of Christ Hellenized out of all recognition. Yet the more we study John's style, the 'feel' of his theology, the nuances of key-words like 'life' and 'glory', the clearer we see that the immediate background of his thinking is the Jewish religion. Old Testament quotations and characters occur everywhere; at point after point we trace the influence of Judaism, sometimes of a rabbinical kind, sometimes of the 'mystical' variety recently found in the Dead Sea Scrolls with their dualism of light and darkness, truth and falsehood, life and death. The 'living Father' of John's Gospel bears no kind of relation to Aristotle's 'unmoved Mover', and his eschatology is undeniably Jewish. Of course he has borrowed from Greek thought. When, for example, we study his idea of 'truth', we are reminded of Plato rather than of Isaiah, for 'reality' rather than 'reliability' is its dominant meaning. (Yet what Platonist would have talked of '*doing* the truth' as John does in 3.21?) Again, Hellenistic religious thinkers of the time made much of the idea of a mediator between God and men, as

[1] W. F. Albright in *The Background of the New Testament and its Eschatology* (ed. Davies and Daube), 153-171.

St John does. And when John sometimes seems to present Christianity as true Knowledge, we remember that contemporary Hellenists liked to think of salvation in terms of *Gnōsis*. Nevertheless, the true roots of John's thinking go deep down into Jewish soil, as they are shaped by the impact on them of the Fact of Christ.

What is St John's relation to the earliest evangel? For an answer all we need do is to direct the reader to C. H. Dodd's *Apostolic Preaching* and his commentary on *The Johannine Epistles*. In these two books he has shown not only that the Fourth Gospel reveals the outline of the apostolic *kerygma* but also that the First Epistle faithfully preserves 'the Gospel' and 'the Commandment' (i.e. the *Kerygma* and the *Didachē*) of the first apostles. It is true that the earliest evangel has, in John's hands, been re-expressed to fit the needs of a much wider spiritual constituency; but, essentially, it is the same preaching and teaching.

Did St John know the Synoptic Gospels? Despite Gardner-Smith's valiant attempt[1] to prove that he did not, it seems very likely that he knew Mark and possibly Luke and Matthew. (Our three most recent commentators in English, Hoskyns, Barrett and Lightfoot, agree on this.) But it is equally clear not only that he used the Synoptic tradition with sovereign freedom, but that he had access to reliable historical traditions of his own. Yet if John used good tradition, as scholars increasingly believe, he wrote not so much as a historian intent on setting down the precise sequence of events as a prophet concerned to declare the ultimate truth of that history.

How does St John stand to St Paul? A few decades ago Deissman could declare that John was Paul's disciple. Few would say this now. St John and St Paul share, of course, common Christian convictions, as all the apostolic writers did. But if one is the disciple of the other, how differently

[1] *St John and the Synoptic Gospels* (1938).

they look at persons, issues, doctrines! Conceive a disciple of Paul who never once uses the verb 'justify' and the noun 'grace' only three times. And where in St John do we find St Paul's characteristic conceptions of the election of Israel, of the New Covenant, and of Christ as the Second Adam? The truth is that St John is not a disciple of Paul at all, but an independent interpreter of Christ with authentic and profound insights of his own.

What, then, did John aim to do in his writings? In the case of the First Epistle the answer is plain. John set himself to refute the Docetists who were troubling the peace of the Church. He did so by passionately reaffirming that the Incarnation—the fact that the Son of God had taken real human flesh—was the roof and crown of Christian truth. But what purpose had he in writing the Gospel? Few people believe now that he wrote to supersede the first three Gospels, or even to correct them. It would be much nearer the mark to say that he wrote to *interpret* them. We have to remember that John was writing not only later than the Synoptists but to men unfamiliar with Jewish terms like Kingdom and Messiah (in which the Gospel had originally been expressed), men who were asking other and more ultimate questions about Jesus and the Gospel. What precise place did Jesus hold in the saving ways of God with men? What was the chief blessing which the Gospel brought to them? How did Jesus remain a living and vital force in the world? It was men like these John had in mind, and questions like these he sought to answer. And what he has done is to bring out the essential and ultimate meaning of the Synoptics. Even in the first three Gospels certain episodes are, so to speak, attempts to convey absolute and eternal truth, e.g. the stories of the Baptism and the Transfiguration. But they occur sporadically, like breaks in the cloud giving us fugitive glimpses of the infinite blue vault of

[1] Heretics who denied the reality of the Incarnation.

heaven. What John did in his Gospel was to show the whole
'sensible' Story of Jesus thus—as the place in history where
the ultimate truth of God is to be found. For him, the Story
is 'an earthly story (and John will have no truck with those
who deny its earthliness) with a heavenly meaning'. But the
'heavenly meaning' is not something arbitrarily superim-
posed on a plain tale which would be better told without it.
It is the true meaning of the earthly story. And the proof
consists in the fact that John's Gospel does make sense of
what we find in the first three. It does give wholeness to
their fragmentariness, so that, as we study it, we are con-
strained to agree with Calvin that the Fourth Gospel is 'the
key which opens the door to the understanding of the first
three'. An interpretation of the Fact of Christ? Yes, the
Fourth Gospel is this in a far higher degree than the Synoptics; but unless Christian experience is the record of one
long and gigantic illusion, it is the right interpretation.

II

CHRISTIANITY ACCORDING TO ST JOHN

If St Paul interpreted the Fact of Christ in terms of righteousness, St John's key-word is *life*. 'All religion,' said
Sabatier, 'is a prayer for life.' In St John's view, God has
answered this prayer in the gift of Christ (John 3.16).

The theme which unifies his Gospel is the theme of life.
Of course, the works and words of Jesus meet a vast variety
of human needs; but through them all runs one single purpose, that of confronting the fact of death, whether of sin
or of the body, with God's answering gift of life in Christ.
'In him was life,' it is written of the *Logos*, and Christ
comes that men 'may have life and have it abundantly'. To
Nicodemus he offers the gift of new birth and eternal life,
as he offers the Samaritan woman 'living water'. He chides

the Jews, 'You will not come to me that you may have life'. To the multitude in Galilee he is life-giving Bread, as in Jerusalem he claims to be the giver of living water. He tells the sorrowing Martha, 'I am the resurrection and the life'. In the Upper Room he claims to be 'the true and living way' to the Father, and assures the disciples, 'Because I live, you shall live also'. And this life-giving Ministry climaxes in the Cross and Resurrection whereby life is made available for all who believe in him.

As for the First Epistle of John, its true sub-title, as Robert Law discerned, would be 'the Tests of Life', because, properly understood, the letter is a series of spiritual criteria for enabling men to know that they have eternal life.

What does St John mean by 'life' or 'eternal life' which he uses interchangeably?[1] It is his equivalent for the presence of the Kingdom of God in the Synoptic Gospels. (Even in the Synoptics 'eternal life' and 'being in the Kingdom' signify the same thing—see Mark 10.17-31). *Zoē aiōnios* means 'the life of the Age (to come)', i.e. the Messianic Age, properly a future blessing. But since the Kingdom has come and the Messiah is here, eternal life has become a blessed reality. Thus, again and again, St John uses the word 'life' for the new quality of life made possible by Christ's coming and the advent of the Spirit. Only once does he essay a definition. 'This is eternal life, that they know thee the only true God, and Jesus Christ whom thou hast sent' (John 17.3). The present tense ('this *is*') shows that eternal life is something to be had even here and now. It consists in *knowing* God, that is, not in theological erudition or in mystical contemplation, but in personal communion with him. It is fellowship with God mediated by

[1] St John uses the word 'life' nineteen times in the Gospel and seven times in I John. 'Eternal life' occurs seventeen times in the Gospel and six times in I John.

Christ who is his Envoy, since no one can come to the Father except through Christ. And it is a *growing* knowledge (*ginōskōsi*)—a 'following on to know the Lord'—only to be perfected hereafter, since the unveiled glory of God is not for flesh and blood.

As we proceed, we shall see how rich is St John's concept of life. Meantime let us compare St Paul and St John.

St Paul sometimes uses the word 'life' for salvation as a present experience (Rom. 6.4, I Thess. 5.10). And both St Paul and St John agree that salvation has been made possible by what God has done for men in Christ. Does their agreement end there?

It is the heart of Paul's Gospel that in the Cross God made Christ 'who knew no sin, to be sin for us, that we might become the righteousness of God in him' (II Cor. 5.21) and that, because of Christ's death for sin, God graciously 'acquits' sinners who put their faith in Christ, giving them a new status with himself. St John declares that God, of his love, gave his Son to live and die for us that, by the new birth and faith, we might have that knowledge of God which is eternal life. So men have said that, whereas in Paul salvation comes by redemption (or reconciliation), in John it comes by revelation. Certainly Paul is more at home in the category of reconciliation, as John is in that of revelation. But let us beware of drawing this contrast too sharply. The man who said, 'God has shone in our hearts to give the light of the knowledge of the glory of God in the face of Christ' (II Cor. 4.6) spoke in accents that St John would have been glad to call his own. Likewise, the man who, in the story of the Foot-washing,[1] taught that there was no room in Christ's fellowship for those not cleansed from sin by his death, was not allergic to the Pauline doctrine of redemption. And in the last analysis how closely Paul and John stand together when they discuss salvation:

[1] E. Hoskyns, *The Fourth Gospel*, 436 f.

PAUL: JOHN:

PAUL:	JOHN:
God shows his *love* for us in that while we were yet sinners Christ died for us (Rom. 5.9).	God so *loved* the world that he *gave* his only Son that whoever *believes* on him should not perish but have *eternal life* (John 3.16).
The *life* I now *live* in the flesh, I live by *faith* in the *Son of God* who loved me and *gave* himself for me (Gal. 2.20).	In this is *love*, not that we loved God but that he loved us and sent his Son to be the *expiation* for our sins (I John 4.10).
The free *gift* of God is *eternal life* in Christ Jesus our Lord (Rom. 6.23).	This is the testimony that God gave us *eternal life*, and this life is in *his Son* (I John 5.11).

But we may underscore the point. It has been alleged that, unlike St Paul, St John teaches no objective doctrine of the Atonement. Will the charge stand? The Christ of St John is a Christ who as the Lamb of God takes away sin (John 1.29) and is an expiation for the world's sins (I John 2.2). He is one who views his death as a vicarious sacrifice needed for men's sanctifying (John 17.19), and the benefit from his 'blood' is cleansing from sin (I John 1.7). A Christ who removes sin, expiating it by his own self-sacrifice and thus purifying sinners who put their faith in him, differs little, if at all, from Paul's Christ. Their terms may vary— John talks much less about the Law and the Flesh, and Life and Light have replaced Righteousness and Reconciliation—but in their basic convictions John and Paul are at one.

For St John, as for the other New Testament interpreters of the Fact of Christ, salvation is a word with three tenses:

'We have passed from death to life' (I John 3.14).
'He that has the Son has life' (I John 5.12).
'Because I live, you will live also' (John 14.19).

But, before we explicate these tenses, let us consider the things from which man needs to be saved.

As in St Paul, they are three—sin, death and the devil—and their sphere is 'the world'. The 'world', originally the good creation of God and still the object of his love (John 3.16), has, by rebellion, become 'human society as it organizes itself apart from God'. There sin, a collective entity (John 1.29, 9.41, etc.), abounds and the devil exerts his power (John 12.31, I John 5.19). Sin is a universal state whose symbol is 'darkness'; and 'if we say we have no sin', we not only delude ourselves but make of no account Jesus Christ who has died to atone for it (I John 1.8, 2.2). Like Paul, John regards sin as 'bondage' (John 8.34; cf. Rom. 7.14); but, whereas Paul connects man's sin with Adam's fall, John simply recognizes its universality as a fact. Again, whereas Paul tends to see sin as a breach of law, John regards it as a hatred of the light—the true light which has streamed into our fallen world through the Son of God (John 9.41, 15.22). Pure and incarnate goodness has been in action among men, and they have repudiated it. Thus the sin of which the Paraclete 'convicts' the world is culpable refusal to believe in Jesus (John 16.9), and once John speaks of Christ's coming almost as Paul did of the Law—its purpose was to throw sin into bold relief (John 15.22). In his First Epistle, where the antinomianism of the heretics is never far from his thoughts, he defines sin as 'lawlessness' (I John 3.4), and he singles out a sin (probably the denial of the Incarnation) so deadly that it puts a man

beyond the pale of that communion with God which is life
(I John 5.16). In the background of sin, as its inevitable
issue if persisted in, stands *thanatos* (death), the fearful
opposite of life (John 5.24, I John 3.14): complete exclu-
sion from him who is 'the fountain of life', an awful synonym for that 'perishing' (John 3.16) of which Judas, 'the
son of perdition', is the supreme illustration. Thus, though
St John does not theorize about sin as St Paul does, no one
may charge him with taking it lightly, or doubt his conviction that Christ has 'overcome the world' (John 16.33)
where sin and death hold sway.

The initial step in salvation St John calls 'passing from
death to life' (John 5.24, I John 3.14). This is no merely
man-willed happening, for no one comes to Christ unless
the Father draws him (John 6.44). God's part in this transition is called 'begetting', as the result for man is new
birth ('born from above', 'born of the Spirit' and 'born
of God' all signify the same thing). 'Unless one is born of
water and the Spirit', Jesus tells Nicodemus, 'he cannot
enter the kingdom of God' (3.5). The reference here is to
Christian baptism, a baptism patterned on Jesus' own baptism as type. True, John never mentions either baptism or
the Eucharist by name; yet the sacraments hold a firm place
in his Christianity. Integral to it is the sacramental principle
that the flesh has become the medium of spiritual life, and
he sees the sacraments as means whereby Christians are in-
corporated in the saving work of him who is the Word made
flesh. Indeed, the probable deeper meaning of his allusion
to the issue of blood and water from the Crucified (John
19.34) is that the sacraments flow from the death of Christ.
In any case, John means the reader in 3.5 to think of the
Christian rite of initiation, a rite which serves as gateway
to the new life and brings the gift of the Spirit.[1]

---

[1] The 'chrism' or 'anointing' of I John 2.20, 27, probably
refers to the gift of the Holy Spirit in baptism.

For John, as for Paul, *faith* is man's way of appropriating
Christ and eternal life. But mark what the count reveals.
Once only does he use the noun 'faith' (I John 5.4), whereas
the verb 'believe' occurs one hundred and seven times.
This can only mean that John conceives faith not as a static
thing, but as a life of energy and growth, in which there is
always more in front of the believer than he has yet been
able to make his own (cf. Phil. 3.12 ff.). As faith comes from
hearing (John 5.24, cf. Rom. 10.14), so its object is Jesus
Christ the Son of God. True faith for John is 'believing
in' (*pisteuein eis*),[1] a phrase without parallel in profane
Greek or the LXX, which John uses no less than thirty-
seven times. To 'believe in' Jesus Christ means to have
confidence in him based on an intellectual acceptance of his
claims. As unbelief means refusal to see God in the incarnate Word, faith is the free response of man to the revelation
of God in him: in existentialist phrase, 'a turning away
from the world and accepting the life that Jesus gives and
is'. Rightly does Bultmann[2] call it 'transition into eschatological existence', since by the decision of faith a man
passes from death to life.

Thus St John's idea of faith, if a little more dogmatic, a
little less gloriously self-abandoning than St Paul's, does not
really differ from it. Sometimes (as in 11.40 and 20.5-9)
'believing' and 'seeing' are linked together, so that faith
appears as a kind of spiritual vision. It is the vision of those
who find God in a historic Person who yet remains for them
the Master-light of all their spiritual seeing.[3]

When, by the Divine drawing of us to Christ, we have

[1] *Pisteuein* c. dative, by contrast, usually connotes simple credence. Thus in John 14.11 'believe me' means 'take my word for
it', whereas 'believe in me' in 14.1 means 'have confidence in me'
as the unique Son of God.

[2] *Theology of the New Testament*, II, 75.

[3] *Note*. John never uses the verb 'believe' to describe Jesus'
relation to the Father. The verb he uses here is 'know'.

made the decision of faith, and, by baptism of 'water and the Spirit', have had the seal set on it, what is the nature of the eternal life we now enjoy? (Here we pass from salvation as a past event to salvation as a present experience.)

No New Testament writer laid hold on the truth of 'realized eschatology' more surely than St John. Only, for the language of 'the Kingdom' he substitutes the language of 'life'. In the Synoptic Gospels Jesus says, 'The Kingdom of God is at hand . . . has come upon you' (Mark 1.15, Luke 11.20). In the Fourth Gospel he says, 'The hour is coming, *and now is*' (John 4.23, 5.25). The words change; the meaning is the same:

'John's formula "the hour cometh and now is", with the emphasis on the "now is", without excluding the element of futurity, is, I believe, not merely an acute theological definition, but is essentially historical, and probably represents the authentic teaching of Jesus as veraciously as any formula could' (C. H. Dodd).[1]

For St. John, then, eternal life is a present boon because Christ has come and died and risen and the Holy Spirit is here, released for men by his dying (John 7.39). This truth he develops in three ways. First, Judgment does not merely come at the end of history; it is, for weal or woe, a present reality (John 3.17-21, 5.22-24). True, God's gift of Christ was designed not for man's doom but for his deliverance, but inevitably men judge themselves by their response to the Fact of Christ. The primary purpose of the sun is not to cast shadows, but it does. So it is with him who is the Light of the world. To accept Christ is to pass out of the range of Judgment; to reject him is to condemn oneself. Judgment is the form salvation takes for those who will have none of it. Second, resurrection is not merely 'then' but 'now'. When Martha affirms that her brother will rise 'at the last day', Jesus rejoins, 'I *am* the resurrection and the

[1] *The Interpretation of the Fourth Gospel*, 447.

life'. There is no denial of a resurrection at 'the last day', but there is an insistence that for those in fellowship with Christ the life to which resurrection leads begins now. 'Your friend is alive now,' Jesus says in effect, 'for in me he touched the life of God which is eternal; in me he had already risen before his body perished' (John 11.25 f. Bernard's paraphrase). Third, without (as we shall see) abandoning the hope of a final coming, St John teaches a return of Christ *in history* through the Resurrection and the coming of the Spirit (John 14.18, 21, 23, 28, 16.16, 22, etc.).

But the cardinal point is that eternal life, the life of God himself, is now offered to men through Christ his Son. 'He who believes in the Son has life' (John 3.36, cf. 6.47 and I John 5.12). Brunner has given this truth a present-day relevance:[1]

'To have part in the divine life of Jesus Christ by faith, to stand in the midst of history and be comprehended in eternal salvation through the reconciliation made in him who is called the Life and the Way to Life—this is to be a Christian—to have life eternal.'

Here, since it closely concerns eternal life (John 17.3), we may glance at St John's concept of *knowledge*. We tend to contrast faith and knowledge—

> *We have but faith, we cannot know,*
> *For knowledge is of things we see,*[2]

but for him they go hand in hand. 'We know and have believed the love God has for us' (I John 4.16, cf. John 6.69, 17.8). Knowledge is the fine flowering of faith, 'intensified and permanent belief which has not yet passed into

[1] *The Theology of Crisis*, 67.
[2] Tennyson, *In Memoriam*.

sight'.[1] 'Believe that you may know and go on knowing,' says Jesus, 'that the Father is in me and I am in the Father' (John 10.38).

The goal of this knowledge is in fact *union with God* through Christ the mediator. Again and again (see especially chapters 10, 14 and 17) Jesus describes a 'mutual indwelling' (or 'coinherence') embracing the Father, the Son and believers. The Father is *in* the Son as the Son is *in* the Father: the Son is *in* believers as believers are *in* the Son. (Similar passages describe a 'mutual knowledge' between the Father, the Son and believers.) Call this 'mysticism', if you will, but it is no conventional kind. 'I had rather be found in Christ than lost in God,' said James Denney. St John would have concurred, for to be 'in the Son' was to be 'in the Father'. The union with God he describes is not only mediated by Jesus Christ, a historical person, but is dynamically conceived and ethically conditioned. Indeed, two strains blend in his doctrine of union with God: one is the idea of the vision of God—'he that has seen me has seen the Father'; the other is the stress on the ethical—'If we love one another, God abides in us'. And these two meet in the concept of *agapē*—the love which gives.

In this world the only sort of union between persons of which we know anything is love; and, says John, this kind of union with a personal God is offered us in Christ. We may imagine it as a spiritual triangle in which the Father, the Son and believers dwell in one another by virtue of a love which is the very life of God. This *agapē*-relation begins in the transcendent world, but it cannot be divorced from this one. Why? Not only because real *agapē* must issue in deeds of brotherly love but also because the crucial deed of *agapē* was enacted in history, outside the northern wall of Jerusalem, on an April day in A.D. 30.[2]

[1] Hoskyns, *The Fourth Gospel*, 303.
[2] This section owes much to C. H. Dodd, *op. cit.*, 187-200.

The imparter of eternal life is the Holy Spirit.

In the Synoptic Gospels Jesus' sayings about the Spirit may be counted on the fingers of one hand. Few as they are, they testify that Jesus promised the Spirit's guidance and power as a gift which his disciples should receive from the Father. St John knew the rich reality of that gift; and if we make due allowance for the commentary of Christian experience, we may fairly hold that his teaching about the Spirit has 'the mind of Christ'. What does he teach?

During his Ministry Jesus was the bearer of the Spirit (John 1.32). Not till he was 'glorified' could the Spirit be given to his followers, and the story of the 'Insufflation' (John 20.21-23) tells how the risen Lord empowered his apostles: 'Receive the Holy Spirit'. We may say that during the Ministry the Spirit was with the disciples in Jesus, but that after the Resurrection Jesus was with his followers through the Spirit (John 14.17). For in John the Spirit is clearly personalized—compare the *ekeinos*, 'he', of the Farewell Discourses with the *touto*, 'this' (Acts 2.33), of Peter on the Day of Pentecost. The Spirit comes as Christ's *alter ego*, not so much to supply his absence as to complete his presence.

Whether it is baptism (John 3.5), the Eucharist (John 6.63) or any true worship (John 4.23), there the Spirit mediates divine life to men. But for fullest light on the Spirit we must turn to the five 'Paraclete' sayings (John 14.16 f., 25 f., 15.26 f., 16.7 ff., 13 ff.). A 'paraclete' is someone called to one's side to give help, so that 'helper' is perhaps the best English equivalent. This future Helper Jesus describes as 'the Spirit of truth' i.e. the Spirit who communicates truth, which for John means knowledge of divine reality. He is sent by the Father in Christ's name to be 'in' the disciples. Them he will 'teach', recalling all that Jesus had said, and enabling them to bear witness to him. He will also 'convince the world of sin and righteousness and judgment' (i.e. show men that *sin* consists in rejecting Jesus, that the only acceptable *righteousness* is that of Jesus—since he has been exalted to God's right hand—and that in the Cross not Jesus but the devil was *judged*). Finally, taking of Christ's things, he will announce things to come (similar are the sayings about the Spirit in I John).

Notice how steadily the Holy Spirit is related to the Fact of Christ. He reminds the disciples of the things Jesus said and did in such a way that something is not merely recalled but now, for the first time, fully understood. What they get is, so to speak, not merely the dream but the dream plus the interpretation. So the Holy Spirit initiates men into the whole meaning of the Word made flesh, acting in their preaching so that the revelation becomes event, and providing the 'eschatological *continuum*'[1] wherein Christ's work, begun in his historic ministry, is wrought out until he comes in glory.

Eternal life is no 'flight of the alone to the Alone'. It is a life lived in the true community, which is the Church.

If the word *ecclēsia* occurs only in III John 6, the idea of the Church dominates John's thinking as truly as it does Paul's. From his Gospel (see chapters 6, 10, 15, 17 and 20 especially) we learn how he conceives of its nature and mission, and in his Epistles we see the Church in the world and at issue with it.

Essentially the Church consists of the men whom the Father has given the Son out of the world (John 17.6), the men who have responded to Christ's call. 'Did I not choose you the Twelve?' says Jesus (John 6.70), and in a scene corresponding to Caesarea Philippi (Mark 8.27 ff.), we hear the new Israel—in nucleus—confessing Jesus to be the Messiah. 'Will you also go away?' 'Lord, to whom shall we go? You have the words of eternal life, and we have believed and have come to know, that you are the Holy One of God'

---

[1] C. K. Barrett's phrase.

(John 6.66-71). This is the Church *in posse*; not till the Christ has risen will it be the Church *in esse*.

Now note the metaphors which describe the nature of the Church. It is the new 'sanctuary of his body', which, by his death and resurrection, he will raise to replace the Jewish temple of stone (John 2.20 ff.). It is God's flock under the Good Shepherd who leads it, feeds it, and lays down his life for it (John 10). It is God's Vine—an ancient symbol for Israel—wherein Christ is the living stock, and the disciples, drawing their life from him, are the branches, called to bear fruit (John 15). Or, again, it is 'a collective Theodore' which the Father has given the Son (John 17.2), a fellowship of the love which has its origin in God (John 17.26).

The mission of the Church is, with the Spirit's help, to proclaim to the world Christ's word (or revelation) and to gather God's true children wherever they are. Its 'notes' are to be universality ('one flock, one shepherd', John 10.16. cf. 11.52) and unity ('that they all may be one' John 17.11, 21). Consecrated by the sacrificial death of its Lord (John 17.17-19) and commissioned to its apostolic task by the risen Christ (John 20.21 f.), the Church is called to show, in its fellowship and by its witness, the one-ness existing between the Father and the Son (John 17.11, 23), and its final destiny is the perfected fellowship of heaven, the Church Triumphant (John 17.24).

Meanwhile on its pilgrim way the Church has its appointed *viaticum*. Though John does not record its institution, the Lord's Supper is the spiritual food of the new life.

If the Word became flesh, material things may become vehicles of spiritual life and truth. This is the principle which underlies John's doctrine of the sacraments, which are means whereby men may share in the saving work of Christ and so possess eternal life. His teaching about the

Eucharist he sets in the context not of the Upper Room but of the Feeding of the Multitude, fitly enough, if the Feeding was indeed a 'Galilean Lord's Supper'. The theme of 6.26-50 is Christ the Bread of Life. Such he is because he 'has come down from heaven' with 'life' for men. Then, at 51b, Jesus proceeds: 'The bread which I will give for the life of the world is my flesh'. Galilee is linked, prophetically, with Golgotha. When the saying mystifies the Jews, Jesus tells them that 'unless they eat the flesh and drink the blood of the Son of man', they cannot 'abide' in him and have eternal life (53 ff.). 'Eating the flesh and drinking the blood of the Son of man' can mean only one thing—the Eucharist. The 'flesh' signifies his manhood 'consecrated' in death for men; the 'blood' his life outpoured for them. To eat and drink them means, by faithful partaking of the emblems of his Passion, to be united to the living Crucified and so share in the divine life he bestows (cf. I Cor. 10.16). It is a high doctrine of the sacrament (though no higher than Paul's); but, as if to guard against any materialistic misconception, we read: 'It is the Spirit that gives life; the flesh is of no avail'. Which is John's way of saying that the efficacy of the rite lies not in the material 'elements' as such, but in the power of the Holy Spirit, the Life-giver.

Finally, eternal life is inescapably ethical (I John 3.14), and never to be dissociated from 'keeping the commandments'. And when we investigate the meaning of this phrase, we find that the commandments really narrow down to one—that of love (*agapē*). This is the divine imperative which flows from the divine indicative which constitutes the Gospel (John 3.16). 'If God so loved us, we also ought to love one another' (I John 4.11). Or, to put it otherwise, love in man's heart is the answer evoked by Divine love, and is to be shown in love of the brethren. 'We love, because he first loved us' (I John 4.19).

This commandment of love, uttered in the Upper Room

(John 13.34, 15.12, 17) and explicated in I John 4 (the Johannine equivalent of I Cor. 13) is the new 'law' for the new Israel. By *agapē*—the love which gives—John means not vague good-will or genial affability, but an active caring for needy brethren (I John 3.17 f.). Thus we show that we are really God's children (I John 4.7). It has been objected that by his talk of 'loving the brethren' John limits the range of love and so falls short of the catholicity of the Sermon on the Mount (Matt 5.43-48). The charge will not really stand, for a love which is response to the universal love of God must itself be universal, and John envisages the widening of the circle of 'the brethren' to embrace all 'the scattered children of God'.

For the rest, the Christian's love is to be patterned on Christ's own: 'As I have loved you' (John 13.34); and our love is to be the badge of our profession to the whole world: 'By this shall all men know that you are my disciples, if you have love for one another' (John 13.35). The sum of the matter is that to abide in love is to abide in God, who is love, and ignorance of love is ignorance of God (I John 4.16). Only love is true churchmanship, and the command of love includes all others. The story they told in the early Church about St John is certainly Johannine. The old man went about repeating, 'Little children, love one another'. And when they asked him, 'Why do you keep saying this?' he answered, 'Because when this is done, all is done'.

It remains to consider salvation as a future hope.

Once men mistakenly supposed that St John had 'de-eschatologized' the Gospel, giving us Christian mysticism instead. There is a 'Not yet' as well as a 'Now' in John's thinking. He has not abandoned the primitive Christian eschatology; but, stripping it of 'the glittering robe of apoc-alyptic' which it at first assumed, he has pierced down to its abiding truth. In this, we believe, he is true to the mind of Christ.

Hoskyns[1] observes that St John 'judges the heart of Christian eschatology to lie less in the expectation of a Second Coming on the clouds of heaven than in the historical Fact of Jesus', which is the appearance of the *eschaton* in time. We have seen the truth of this. But, for all his stress on 'realized eschatology', St John never abandons his hope of a final *dénouement*. Thus, in both Gospel and Epistle, he looks for a 'last day' (John 6.39, 40, 44, 54, I John 4.17), a Coming of Christ (John 14.3, 21, 22, I John 2.28) with resurrection and judgment (John 5.29, 12.48, I John 4.17) and final bliss for the redeemed (John 14.3, 17.24, I John 3.2).

But he sees this *dénouement* rather as the finalizing of present realities (e.g. judgment) and the visible unfolding of what now is (Christ's glory, for example); and though he holds fast to the hope of a final 'manifestation' of Christ in glory, he views the *Parousia* also as a continuing 'Presence' (which is what *Parousia* means) inaugurated by the Passion.

When we study eternal life as a future hope, we find him building on the same base as Paul—the strong love of God in Christ. John 10.28 f. corresponds to Rom. 8.35-39. 'I am giving them eternal life,' says Jesus, 'and they shall never perish, and no one shall snatch them out of my hand.' Christ's hand, as the next verse shows, is the Father's hand. As in Paul, Christ's love is the love of God (Rom. 8.35, 39), so, in John, Christ's grasp upon his own is the Father's grasp, and invincible. The disciples may in this world suffer loss, anguish and death, but in the end they will still be safe; for they are in the loving hand of the Divine Shepherd and cannot be torn from its keeping. Similarly in John 11.25 f. Jesus tells Martha: 'I am the resurrection and the life; he who believes in me, though he die, yet shall he live'. Because the life which Jesus gives and is, is God-given life, it is indestructible and will survive the shock of death and be perfected

[1] *Op cit.*, 268.

in heaven. In his 'Father's house', Jesus tells his disciples, 'are many rooms', and he is but going ahead to prepare for their entrance (John 14.2 f.). The background of this saying may well be Mark 14.12-16 where the disciples were sent ahead to make ready a guest chamber or upper room. They 'did not know the way', but followed the owner, as Jesus had said, and found everything 'prepared'. So, in the Fourth Gospel, the disciples' errand of the previous day has become a parable of eternity, and the Upper Room had been made to foreshadow the home of God.[1]

As Paul conceives the life hereafter as a family life (Rom. 8.29), so John stresses the *social* aspect of the Christian hope. 'I desire,' Jesus prays in the Upper Room, 'that they also, whom thou hast given me, may be with me where I am, to behold my glory' (John 17.24). This is pure eschatology: it is a prayer that the Church Militant may become the Church triumphant. We may leave the last word to St John in his First Epistle: 'Beloved, we are God's children now; it does not yet appear what we shall be, but we know that when he appears, we shall be like him, for we shall see him as he is. And everyone who thus hopes in him purifies himself as he is pure' (I John 3.2 f.). All the essentials of a true Christian hope are here: the saving relationship to God on which all rests; the *nescio, nescio quæ iubilatio* which must ever be man's last word on the felicity of heaven; the certainty that the last end of the believer is the Beatific Vision—to see the Lord and to be like him—and the final stress on Christian hope as a sanctifying virtue.

III

THE CHRIST OF ST JOHN

Who does St John conceive Jesus Christ to be? The short

[1] H. M. Foston, *The Evening of the Last Supper*, 39-44.

answer is: the Divine Son of God who, embodying in himself God's saving purpose, took human flesh for us men and for our salvation and by his death has given us life.

'He sees everything from the Divine side,' said Westcott of St John. This is specially true of Christ's person. Yet if John is sure of Christ's Divinity, he is no less sure of his humanity. Hence his portrait of Jesus Christ, with its wonderful blending of majesty and lowliness: on the one hand, the royal dignity of one who knows himself to be the unique Son of God, speaking the accents of Deity incarnate, and, on the other, one who is truly human and wears the form of a Servant: the portrait indeed sketched in miniature in the *Pedilavium*:

'Jesus, knowing that the Father had given all things into his hand, and that he had come from God and was going to God, rose from supper, laid aside his garments, and girded himself with a towel. Then he poured water into a basin, and began to wash the disciples' feet . . .' (13.3-5).

Every reader notices how strikingly Christ's person dominates the Fourth Gospel by contrast with the first three where Jesus keeps his Messiahship a secret till the end and only in private, to his disciples, speaks of his unique relationship to the Father. Yet John's conception of Christ is essentially a working out of Christological hints that lie undeveloped in the first three evangelists, and we shall understand it better if we recall two things. We must first remember the vantage-point from which John views Christ's person. It is at once post-Resurrection, post-Pentecost and post-Pauline. John's Christ is not only the Christ who came preaching in Galilee; he is Jesus Christ the risen Lord; he is the omnipresent Saviour who, through the Holy Spirit, has returned to company with his People; he is that immeasurably great person who had so filled the world of Paul and the other apostles with his power and presence that they were compelled to set him on that side of reality we call

Divine and to think of him in cosmic terms. The other thing
to remember is that the 'raw materials' of a very high
Christology are there, to begin with, in the Synoptic
Gospels. If it be true that in the first three Gospels 'the
Kingdom of God is Christ himself', who can he be who
incarnates the Kingdom? Moreover, even in the Synoptic
Gospels Jesus affirms his sufficiency to be the Saviour of
sin-burdened men and claims a unique Sonhood to God.
John's Christology is an expanding, in terms of Christian
experience, of such things as these. More clearly than the
other evangelists, as clearly as Paul himself, he saw that
Jesus is the Gospel, and the Gospel is Jesus.

With these things in mind, we will content ourselves with
considering three aspects of John's Christology.

Let us take, first, the seven great parables of his person,
which John sets on the lips of Jesus. Are these purely Johannine constructions? In their range and richness they trans-
cend anything in the first three Gospels, but they are not
without parallels there. The Christ who said, 'Come unto
me, all you who labour and are heavy laden, and I will give
you rest', and 'This is my body', is not very different, if
we allow for the commentary of Christian experience, from
the Christ who says, 'I am the Bread of Life' and 'I am
the true Vine'. The seven 'I am's' are of course couched
in John's own idiom; yet they attest the spiritual impact
which the living Christ had made on John and his friends
for two generations. Though sixty years have passed since
Jesus returned to the unseen world, he has been with his
own, through the Spirit, proving himself the very bread of
hungry souls, the one true light in a dark world, the good
shepherd leading and feeding God's flock in Asia as once
in Galilee, the bringer of life to men in dread of death, the
one real way to that ultimate reality men call God. Unless
Christian experience is a liar, this is important testimony to
who Christ is.

Next, let us note those sayings of Jesus in the Fourth Gospel which claim a unique unity with the unseen Father. If St John has shaped them as we now have them, he is but developing something which is rooted in the Synoptics and goes back to Jesus himself. A Synoptic 'point' has become in John a 'star'. What they assert is, on the Father's side, complete confidence in his Well-beloved, and, on Christ's, an unclouded open-ness of the mind of the Son to the Father, resulting in a profound unity of will and purpose and indeed in a mystical co-inherence:

'The Father loves the Son and has given all things into his hand' (3.35).

'The Son can do nothing of his own accord but only what he sees the Father doing . . . for the Father loves the Son and shows him all that he himself is doing' (5.19 f.).

'My Father is working still, and I am working' (5.17).

'I and the Father are one' (10.30).

And this unity with the Father reaches sublimest expression in the Upper Room as Jesus prays for believers that 'they all may be one, even as thou, Father, art in me, and I in thee, that they all may be one in us' (17.21). The person who so speaks is, for the man who writes of him, one who comes from the very depths of the being of God himself.

We turn, finally, to the *titles* of Jesus in St John. It goes without saying that John believed Jesus to be the Messiah; but if proof were necessary, we need only turn to the first chapter of his Gospel where, after the Prologue, he calls the roll of Jesus' Messianic titles. It is a mark of the Fourth Gospel's fidelity to the primitive tradition that in it Jesus styles himself nearly a dozen times by the majestic but mysterious title of 'Son of man', for the title must have conveyed little to many of his readers. What is said about the Son of man in the Fourth Gospel? Two main things: first, that he descends from heaven (3.13, 6.62); and, second, that his destiny is to be 'lifted up' or 'glorified' (3.14, 8.28, 12.23, 13.31) before he 'ascends where he was before' (Here we recall how in the Synoptics the title has two main motifs attached to it—suffering and sovereignty; but in John the suffering is the sovereignty, the Son of man's glory is the Cross.) Once the Son of man appears as men's God-appointed judge (5.27). But perhaps the most impressive of all John's Son of man sayings comes in 1.51 (based on the Bethel story of Gen. 28) where the disciples are promised an opened heaven and the angels ascending and descending on the ladder of the Son of man. What does this mean? Jesus—the visible, historical man Jesus—'is the place of revelation, the place over which the heaven has been opened'.[1]

The third title, the Son of God, is that into which John pours his profoundest thought about Christ. The concordance shows that in the Gospel and Epistles Jesus appears as the Son of God no less than forty-three times. Sometimes it is 'the Son of God' or 'his [God's] Son'; often it is 'the Son' *simpliciter*; and in a few cases it is 'his only [*monogenēs*] Son'. Occasionally 'the Son of God' may mean no more than 'Messiah', but in most passages the suggestion is of a relationship to God only to be described as uniquely filial. Here is another Synoptic 'point' become a 'star' in John; for these Johannine references are but expansions of the claim to unique Sonhood found in the Great Thanksgiving (Matt. 11.25-27-Luke 10.21-22) and the parable of the Wicked Vinedressers (Mark 12.1-12). Join these sayings about the Son with those in which Jesus claims pre-existence (e.g. 8.58) or in which he uses the accents of Deity (*ego eimi*, 8.24, 28, 13.19), and we see that the relation between Jesus and God is an eternal one. It is also, as John makes

[1] Hoskyns, *op. cit.*, 183.

abundantly clear, one of love. What does this mean but that the human life of Jesus is the projection of that eternal relation of love upon the plane of history? The love the Father had for the Son 'before the foundation of the world' (17.24) is to be seen working in the life, death and resurrection of Jesus. And this love, thus manifested in history, is meant to bring men into that unity of which the Father-Son relationship is the eternal archetype.

So we come back, at the end, to the title with which John begins his Gospel—the Word (*Logos*) made flesh. Endless research has been done on its antecedents. Scholars have explored its origins in the creative Word of God in the Old Testament, the Word of the Lord which came to the prophets, the concept of Wisdom (Proverbs 8) and the rabbis' hypostatisation of the *Torah*. On the Greek side, they have traced the idea back through the *Logos Spermatikos* of the Stoics to Heracleitus of Ephesus. While grateful for their researches, we must avoid the 'genetic fallacy' of supposing that to know all this is to understand completely what John means. *John started from the Fact of Christ*. He was looking for a category which would worthily express its meaning to all men, Jews and Greeks. Familiar and ready to hand lay the concept of the Word or *Logos*, freighted with a proper theological significance for his purpose.

What he seeks to say by it is that the only proper perspective in which to see the Story of Jesus is a Divine one (hence he begins in God's eternity) and that Jesus Christ is God's saving purpose for men in terms of a human life. The Word (so the Prologue argues) is God's creative and redeeming Purpose. By this Word all things were made. It was manifested in the world as life and light, the light open to every man born. When mankind as a whole failed to welcome this Word, God sent it to Israel through the prophets. Israel too rejected the Word, save for a faithful few. Finally, God incarnated his Word in a human being, who was his unique Son.

In the person and work of Jesus of Nazareth, then, the saving Purpose of God was embodied. He is the dynamic and redemptive Word of God. He has made plain God's gracious mind and purpose, and that purpose is one of holy love in action for men's salvation, which is eternal life. This is the ultimate meaning of the Fact of Christ.

EPILOGUE

Our theme has been the Fact of Christ and its explication by its first interpreters. But the process of interpretation did not stop with St John. It went on.

In the first few centuries we see the Gospel in process of being re-defined in Greek terms and categories; the making of the creeds; the development of the new Israel into the Catholic Church. The process of re-definition is difficult and dangerous—so fatally easy is it to change the Gospel into something quite different that an Athanasius has to refuse all compromise with an Arius, if the truth is to be maintained. Moreover, new terms are found for old truths: Jesus the Messiah becomes God the Son; the Holy Spirit, God the Holy Ghost; and the doctrine of the Trinity, there in germ from the start, emerges clearly.

At the Reformation we see not only the removal of false accretions but the re-discovering of important New Testament truths in peril of being forgotten. Luther recovers Paul's great doctrine of justification by faith in danger of being submerged beneath a theology of merit. Calvin goes back to the early Fathers of the Church, and systematizes the new insights of the Reformers.

The process of interpretation still goes on. It always must, as men's thought-world changes, if the Fact of Christ is to come livingly home to men in their own day. In our time the most daring proposal, that of Bultmann, has been for a 'demythologizing' of the Gospel and its re-statement in terms of Existentialism. The intention to state the Gospel in modern terms is laudable, but it is fraught with peril, the peril of corrupting the Gospel. Bultmann undertakes to give us Christianity without tears, but what he gives us is tears without Christianity.[1] But if we reject his methods, we cannot shirk the challenge which he seeks to force.

Now, as in New Testament times, the Church lives between D-Day and V-Day, when the complete meaning of what God did in Christ will be unveiled. Of this consummation we can speak only in myths and symbols. And here the Seer of Revelation, whom space has not allowed to be heard, may be allowed the last word:

' I saw a new heaven and a new earth.'

' They shall hunger no more, neither thirst any more; the sun shall not strike them, nor any scorching heat. For the Lamb in the midst of the throne will be their shepherd, and he will guide them to springs of living water; and God will wipe away every tear from their eye.'

' And they shall reign for ever and ever.'

Then the Fact of Christ will need no more interpreting.

[1] Oral tradition credits T. W. Manson with this *mot*.

INDEX OF SUBJECTS

INDEX OF AUTHORS

INDEX OF BIBLICAL PASSAGES